40 Years in the Wilderness:

The Making of a Man

Presented to:

_____

By

_____

40 Years in the Wilderness

The Making of a Man

A Literary Memoir

of

Marriese Alexander Jones, Sr.

Stories and reflections

that will feed the soul

40 Years In The Wilderness: The Making Of A Man

Published by McClain Productions
Longmont, Colorado
Printed in the United States

ISBN: 978-1975869281

All scripture quotations are taken from The Holy Bible, New International Version. Copyright @ 1973, 1978, 1984 by International Bible Society.

First Printing: August 2017

Illustrations: Carrie Martin

Marriese Alexander

Meaning of Name

Dark-Skinned Warrior

The Calling

Isaiah 6:1

"Then I heard the voice of the LORD saying, 'Whom shall I send? And who will go for us? "
And I said, 'Here am I. Send me!'"

Contents

Dedication   i

Acknowledgments   iii

Epigraph   xi

Preface   xiii

Foreword   xvii

Prologue   xix

Introduction   xxvii

Part I - Memories of a Young Marriese

Chapter 1 - My World of Tears   1

Chapter 2 - Fishing   25

Chapter 3 - Grandma's Kitchen   27

Chapter 4 - The Shoes   31

Chapter 5 - A Night Like No Other 35

Chapter 6 - Shattered   41

Part I - Reflections   47

Chapter 7 - A Broken Heart   49

Part II-Memories of Marriese as a Teen and Young Man

Chapter 8 - Anger   59

Chapter 9 - Locked Up   63

Chapter 10 - The Streets of Miami 69

Chapter 11 - My 3:00 AM Meeting with God 75

Part II - Reflections   81

Chapter 12 - A Mighty River Begins to Flow 83

Chapter 13 - All Things New   89

Chapter 14 - Called Into the Army of the Lord 93

Part III - Memories of Mo Jones

Chapter 15 - A Restaurant and a Movement   101
Part III Reflections - A Wise Marriese Looks Ahead...113
Chapter 16 - Water & Fishing   115
Chapter 17 - He Is My Mouthpiece   119
Chapter 18 - For Such a Time as This   125
Chapter 19 - The Last Hour   139
Chapter 20 - Not for My Glory but Yours   149
The Calling   163
Epilogue and Photos   164

Appendices

Appendix I - The Anointed BBQ and Soul Food
    The Anointed Story...
    Anointed Customer Comments...
    News Articles About Anointed BBQ

Appendix II - Hedges and Highway Outreach Ministries
    Our Structure for Reconciling People & Communities

Appendix III - Credentials
    Credentials
    Contact Information

Dedication

I dedicate this book to my mother, Geraldine Jones, the bravest person I have ever known, my best friend and my number one supporter in my world. I thank you Mama for giving me life, for all your many sacrifices and for your enduring love which I was not to know fully until I was grown, because you never did want the focus to be on you.

****

I dedicate this book to God, who I love more than anyone. You called me to yourself when I was just a young boy, taking me on a forty-year journey to make me into a man. God, you are my father and your hand in my life has been my greatest joy.

Those forty years meant traveling through the wilderness of suffering, grief and sorrow, as well as through mountain-top experiences and peaceful valleys. When no one else would help me, you taught me that if I called your Name you would come running. You have never failed me. You are my strong tower, my fortress, my refuge, my strength, my defender, my avenger, my advocate, my rock, my hope, my truth, my comforter, my light, the King of Glory, the LORD of Hosts, the LORD Almighty, my Redeemer.

And you have been by my side all the days of my life.

I thank you for your Holy commission to be a soldier in the army of the LORD and for the glorious calling to make you known to the people today.

I could not have written a better story for my life.

God, I will never stop boasting of your faithfulness. I will never stop singing your praises. You saved me and preserved me. I thank you for catching every tear that I ever shed and for turning them into a mighty river that now rages for your GLORY.

My life is yours.

"I knew you before I formed you in your mother's womb. Before you were born I set you apart and appointed you as my prophet to the nations."
—Jeremiah 1:5

In Loving Memory of Riley Short.

In the brief time that I knew you, you were like a son to me and I loved you as a son. You were only 16 years old when God took you home. Your spirit will live on forever at Anointed BBQ and Soul Food

Acknowledgments

I thank God for my wonderful family. To everyone in the Jones family and to everyone who knows they ARE family, I love you for every part you have played in my life. You are woven permanently into the armor that God has designed for me to wear in this life and I am beyond grateful.

I am deeply indebted to my Grandmother Maggie Jones, who through her undying love, courage and care taught her family of seventeen children, forty-seven grandchildren, one-hundred eleven great grandchildren and ninety-nine great, great grandchildren the true meaning of what it means to LOVE without conditions. Grandmother your love, legacy and food lives on through me and now through *Anointed BBQ & Soul Food* and every person who has had the "Anointed Experience." More than that, Grandmother your example of loving people just as they are has pierced my heart. May I always be an example to everyone I meet of your

Great Love.

Maggie Lee Jones

I thank God for my beautiful children, Marriese, Jr., Ty, Dekarri, Jaiden, Donell, Chonna, Naya, Amarri, Danielle and my 7 grandchildren You are all my heritage and my portion from the LORD.

A Special Thanks...

To McDivitt Jones. You are first on my list to thank and there are no words that can ever capture the value of our lives of 40 years, bonded together from the beginning. You were always there for me in my darkest nights and we are one soul.

A special thank you to my son, Marriese Jr., my namesake. Thank you, son, for the last two years of being by my side. You always were there for your pops and I love having you around. You are raising a beautiful family and have given me three grandchildren: Kaiden Jones, Kaidence Jones, and Marriese Amir Jones. I am infinitely proud.

To my son Donell. You are a strength and encouragement to me. All these years, I have watched you grow into an incredible man. Being your father is a true blessing and extra portion of the LORD. You make me so proud, son.

A special thank you to my son, Ty. I am so proud of the man you have become and all that you are doing, including the family you are raising!

To my son, Dekarri. You have grown into a great man. After reading this story, I hope you can see that I wanted you to be strong and independent, like my father wanted for me. You are such a wonderful man. You have my heart son, now and forever.

To my son, Jaiden. You were just one year old when I came into your life. You are God's gift to me and I want us always to stay close. I love you Jaiden, forever. I am proud of the man you arc becoming.

An additional thanks to my first born, my daughter, Chonna. Thank you for coming to Colorado and working long days by my side. It was a great experience and one of my dreams to have you and my children benefit from all of my hard work to build a legacy for my kids and grandkids. Thank you for my granddaughter, Seyvn and I cannot wait to meet my next granddaughter, Goldyn, in October 2017.

A special thank you to my daughter, Naya. You have accomplished so much in your young life and your trip to Colorado meant so much to me, although I am not good at taking the time for myself personally to be with those I love. I will get better at that. I love you Naya, from the bottom of my heart.

To Danielle. I thank God for you Mooka. I love you with all my heart and it is a privilege to be your father.

A special thank you to my daughter, Amarri. You came in December and helped me so much. I am so proud of you and love you so much, Mari.

To Arthur Jones. You are what it means to be family. For all that you have given me endlessly and how you believed in me over all the years, I thank you Uncle. You have always been there.

To Bridgette Davis. You are my daily supporter and Anointed's very best manager. I thank God for you every day. Thank you for believing in me. We are family.

To Rusty Collins. What you did for me in opening your home to me and my family for over a year means more to me than all the money in the world. You believed in me, encouraged me, counseled me and stood by my side. You are a true brother.

To John (Tommy) Sellers. You were my sidekick and the one who stuck by me since Anointed's first day. You carried me through. I could not have done it without you.

To Alan Jones, my uncle and great supporter. A special thanks to you Uncle for always being there for me.

To Angie Spell. My first wife and the mother of our three wonderful children. You put up with me while I was on drugs and in the streets for so many years. You tried everything to help me. You are a great woman and I thank you for being an outstanding mom to our children. Your continued support in my life is one of God's blessings to me.

To three of my greatest supporters, dear friends and volunteers: Lori Schroeder, Louella House and Mary Ellen. I couldn't imagine being on this journey without each of you.

To Toniette Stokes. A special thank you for carrying me through many months when Anointed first opened. We have known each other since we were teenagers and you were Anointed's first Cook and Manager. You were a huge part of Anointed's beginning days and I am so grateful for all that you sacrificed for me.

To Uncle Johnny from Miami. A special thanks to you. You have always been there for me to encourage me and believed in me, pressing me to never give up.

To my sister Donna Smith. How can I ever put into words how much you mean to me? Thank you for never giving up on me. I am blessed that you are my sister.

To Paul and Deidre Barnes. I met you when we first came to Colorado. You have been my true friends through everything. We will always be family and I love you both. Thank you for never giving up on me.

To my spiritual father, Bishop William Moore, and my spiritual mother, Sandra Gibson, from Alabama. You mean more to me than you will ever know and your impact in my life continues to grow.

To Sam and Sholanda Adams. How incredible it has been to journey with you. I love you both, you are family!

To my siblings: Johnnie P. Waters, Terry Jones, William Lester, Angela Poole and Victoria Davis. Your presence in my life and encouragement continues to ground me. I thank God for each one of you.

To Valerie Davis, who was my very best-friend and wife for 13 years. We endured so much together. I will never forget how you encouraged me, believed in me, travelled all over the country with me, trusted me and prayed with me. Thank you for all that you gave me including the incredible chance to raise our boys with you. They mean so much to me. You are a wonderful mother and you deserve life's greatest happinesses.

To Sylvia B. Johnson-Matthews. You treated me like your own. During my darker days you were my constant encouragement. You love me without conditions. I am forever grateful. You are a spiritual mother to me and you are loved continuously.

To my cousins, Demetri Simmons and Rodney Jones. A special thanks goes to you, family, for your constant encouragement during many hard days of my journey.

To Sylvia Parks Johnson. You know that you were always a special blessing in my life and my family. You were like my own Godmother.

To Carlton and Erma Harris. You will always be my in-laws and I love you.

To my dear cousins, Maggie Jones and Yashica Godbolt. You have been some of my greatest supporters.

To Victoria Jones, my cousin. A special thanks to you for being a blessing in my life.

To Robert and Tammy Montgonery, Rodney and Lisa Jones, and Leroy and Rosa Jones. You are FAMILY. You all mean more to me than I could write in this book.

To Reverend Louis Davis and Sister Selena. You have encouraged me as a Prophet and helped me in my many endeavors over the years. How grateful I am to you.

To Francine Collins, Danielle and Donell Robertson, Faheem Willis, Michelle and Ed Langford, Linda Montoya Pastor, Kathleen Sargeant, and Christy Robertson. Thank you for all of your support and encouragement over the years.

A very special thanks to Derek Hines, Ken Brawley and all the people who allowed me to dump pressure on during those hard days and nights of endless struggle once I arrived in Denver.

To Michael Schweiger and the entire class of Reggie Moore at Denver Seminary in 2016. Thank you for your unconditional love and friendship and for helping me discover the meaning of my name, Dark-Skinned Warrior.

To Jim and Stacy McDonald. For years you believed in me when no one else did, listening to my dreams and visions. Thank you for never giving up on me.

To Bill and Mike Hoff of Corporate Properties. A special thank you for all of the years of talks and seeing me through. You are not forgotten.

To Mr. Bud, who came along ***Anointed's*** path in the final push before opening. Your expertise and skills allowed the restaurant to be operational. You provided your resources to me at a fraction of the cost and became my advisor. You are a great friend to me and I am grateful.

To my Family Leadership Training Institute (FLTI) class and Colorado State University. You encouraged me and believed in me. I am grateful for the incredible program of FLTI and the friendships I made along the way.

To the Colorado Rockies and especially Jim Kellogg. Thank you for your continued support over the years of my non-profit, Hedges and Highway Outreach Ministries. Your generosity has made an enormous impact in the community that we serve.

And finally a special thank you to ***Anointed BBQ & Soul Food's*** angel, Shirleen Ratliff. You and your husband Bud built this building back in the 1950's and you operated it as a restaurant known as "The Hobo." Today, over 60 years later, it is serving the community again in so many ways. We are feeding the people's bodies and souls. It is because of your belief in me, your generosity, your working with me on paying the rent, that any of this has been able to happen. Nothing with ***Anointed*** would have been possible without your support. You believed in me when the building still needed so much work and I had no money. You kept encouraging me to keep going and even found resources to help. The restaurant you built is once again a lighthouse for the people of Sheridan and all of Colorado. Thank you, Ms. Shirleen. We love you.

Epigraph

It Don't Hurt Now
Teddy Pendergrass

*It used to be every night
I would cry my heart out over you,
It used to be every day
I would wish you here close to me.
I couldn't sleep, couldn't eat,
I'd just sit at home and I'd weep,
but now all that has changed,
I've found someone to ease my pain
And it don't (hurt now no not now)
baby it don't hurt now (no not now)
well there's no more sleepless nights
no more heartaches, no more fights,
and it don't (hurt now, not now)
It used to be every time
I would hear a sad song, I would die.
I couldn't sleep, couldn't eat,
I'd just sit at home and I'd weep,
but now all that has changed,
I've found someone to ease my pain
(And it don't) nooooo (hurt now, no not now)
trying to tell you, (baby it don't hurt now,
no not now)
Well there's no more sleepless nights
no more heartaches and no more fights,
(and it don't hurt now) no it don't (not now) yeah
See there's no more sleepless nights
no more heartaches and no more fights
now all that has changed
I've found someone to ease my pain (And it don't) nooo (hurt now,
no not now)
trying to tell you it don't (hurt now) no (no not now)
see there's no more sleepless nights no more heartaches and no
more fights and it don't (hurt now) no it don't (not now)*

xi

*Will you listen to me please please
trying to tell you that it don't don't...No it don't hurt no more, I
think it's over,I think it's over I think it's over ...Don't hurt now... it's
over between me and you, Don't hurt now between me, Don't hurt
now
tired being alone, Don't hurt now-yes I am-tired of sitting all alone
Don't hurt now, don't hurt now
think I can make it -I think I-Don't hurt now I think I can make it
without you, think I can make it-Don't hurt now think I can make
it Don't hurt now yes I can. I don't need you no Don't hurt now
more, I don't need you no more, I don't need you, I don't need you
no more. No No No No No No I'm a grown man, yes I am, think I can
understand yes I can, that you didn't mean me no good, and right
now in my heart (Don't hurt now)I'm so happy, I'm so happy (Don't
hurt now).*

****

**Jesus, I used to hurt so bad and cry every day! I
couldn't understand why you were not here close to
me. But Jesus it don't hurt now. You knew. You knew!**

**You were there all along.
And Jesus it don't hurt now.
Do not feel bad for me.
Rejoice!
Because I made it through...
And it don't hurt now.**

-*Marriese Jones*

Preface

40 Years in the Wilderness: The Making of a Man is a literary memoir about a boy, Marriese Jones, Sr., growing up in the town of Goulds, southwest of Miami, in the late 60's and early 70's; a teen then living on the streets of Miami and an older, wiser Mo who is looking back and making sense of his life.

This book begins in the Prologue, to which the goal is to set the stage with an accurate historical and cultural context allowing the story to progress with what really happened, unfiltered. The reader is invited to travel to the story's time and place (Goulds, Florida). Our lens, or worldviews will always affect how we interpret life events and that is based on our own experiences growing up. The reader is asked to be aware of our lens we use to interpret the literary piece in our hands. If possible, the reader is invited to put on the lens of Marriese A. Jones, Sr. to allow for a richer understanding of the journey he travelled.

Part I begins with Chapter 1 and the memories of young Marriese, from the time of five through his twelfth birthday, (1968-1980) as if a character in a narrative form. The main character, the boy Marriese, takes you along his journey. This allows you to have as close to an accurate experience as possible with him and his childhood as he remembers it. As he lived with daily childhood abuse and trauma, you will experience what it was like be there with him, running along the paths as he is picking up bottles and cans, dodging bodies, crime, pimps and drug dealers. Part I concludes with an essay of Marriese's reflections, done by a slightly older teen. This voice of the teenager will then continue into Part

II, in which he recalls experiences that span the next ten years of his life.

The next ten years include rebellion, living the life of a thug of crime in the rough inner-city of Miami and his eventual arrest and time in prison. Life was hard during those days. It was all about survival for Marriese during these years and about the hustle. God is present for Marriese throughout those ten years and begins to pull Marriese to his unique calling. On one life altering night, God calls Marriese by a new name, revealing to him the vocation that God had designed for him before his birth. God redeems Marriese's future in one night's revelation and all that Marriese thought he had lost over the years. Section II will conclude like Section I, with reflective essays that will be told from a man who is raising a family and being transformed by God for the next 12 years.

The book concludes Part III with the materializing of one of Marriese's promises from God and the documentation of the birth of his dream restaurant, *Anointed BBQ & Soul Food.* Section III ends with a Reflection like Sections I & II, but this time with the voice of the present day "Mo" reflecting on his life as he discovers of deep truths and making sense of his past, but this time he is looking ahead to his future. Marriese's story spans decades of his life. Thus, his journey is organized into Sections I-III, and includes both Memories and Reflections.

Writing this memoir reaches deep into Marriese's person as he recounts his journey which includes an historical and spirit filled analysis in a story form. This helps to make sense of his self and his world as he knew it then and knows it now. We as the reader will follow how a young boy dealt with tragedy and how a man filtered that trauma into a daily grid so he may grow up and have all that we all long for as humans: love, family, relationships, and a meaningful and purpose driven life experience. You will ride the experiences with Marriese, (Mo) with intimate moments into very tender parts of his childhood while you feel his story with all the emotional truths that he embraces.

Imagination will play a part in this narrative, as Mo recounts for you some memories scarred by heartache and extreme sorrow. We give him grace to allow for the fallibility of the memory if some facts are not exact. We understand the reshaping of time when telling a story and we give him that grace that this is not a factual recording but his attempt to remember and re-create an experience for you so he can convey deep truths to us as the reader about the power of God to rescue, restore and revive even the worst situations. A theme of God's faithfulness emerges throughout Marriese's life and God's reliability can be found among his essay reflections. We understand the reshaping of time when telling a story.

We embrace that this memoir will reveal to us something. We are on a path of discovery first with the young Marriese in Part I and next with the teenage Marriese in Part II of the Memoir, who are more naïve who don't understand quite as much of what is happening. Part III shows a wiser and older Mo uncovering the meanings God has given to him over the years of his life story that were not available to the younger boys. However, all are powerful in their own right.

We will all learn something here. Something of Mo , something of our world and something of ourselves. The lines are not black and white, but somewhat blurred at times. But is that not what life is really? We like to make life clear cut, however life is messy. And people are messy. In this life, we are called to experience each other's humanness, embracing our frailties, and celebrating each other's successes and carrying one another's burdens. Here, on these pages, we experience another's mind and understand that this life was not chosen by him but given to him. We carry just a bit of his burden with us now, relieving his pain as we do. He finally can share with the world. We will experience how he coped and overcame. He speaks truth to us. And I, for one, am grateful, for I have been changed forever. And, so will you be. I would like to see any of us do any better. I don't believe it would ever be possible.

Foreword

Mo Jones: A Man of Fortitude

Fortitude. The word is a noun. It stands on its own accord. By definition it means COURAGE during times of pain or adversity. To elaborate on this great word, we see that the word actually means BRAVERY, ENDURANCE, RESILIANCE, BACKBONE, SPIRIT, GRIT, STEADFASTNESS, MORAL FIBER, STRENGTH OF CHARACTER, STRONG-MINDEDNESS, STRENGTH OF MIND, and in fact, just plain GUTS.

This is the perfect definition of Mo Jones.

A boy with GUTS & ENDURANCE.

A teen with BRAVERY & RESILIANCE.

A young man with BACKBONE & SPIRIT.

A father with STEADFASTNESS & MORAL FIBER.

A Man of STRENGTH OF CHARACTER & STRENGTH OF MIND.

It's as if the enemy of God knew that this man's story would be great from the time he was a little boy.

It is as if the enemy of God was determined to wreck Mo Jones and attack him right down to his core making every effort to ensure that Mo believed he was in fact the exact opposite of who GOD ORDAINED HIM TO BE.

It is as if the enemy of God used deadly strategies to attack especially Mo's mind of all things because God had in fact ordained Mo's mind to be STURDY AND FULL OF STRENGTH.

It's as if God said to the enemy, "Go ahead and try as you will, for you will see that my son cannot be deceived with your lies of trauma to the point of destroying him or his hope in me or his future."

It's as if God said to the enemy, "Go ahead and try as you will, for you will see that my son cannot be weak or believe that he will never amount to anything, for he is made in my image and I have put a spirit of FORTITUDE in him that will prevail beyond anything you have ever seen and the truth of who he is as my chosen one for he will prevail."

It's as if God said to the enemy, "Go ahead and try as you will, for you will see that my son is a man that will not be stopped, for he will be my mouthpiece and my banner and your plans to destroy him will only strengthen him to the point of becoming a bronzed soldier in my army."

It's as if God himself hand crafted Mo's life story of hardships, at least that is what it seems. But you dear reader, see for yourself. For this is Mo Jones and this is his story.

Anonymous

Prologue

Life in Goulds
The Deep South

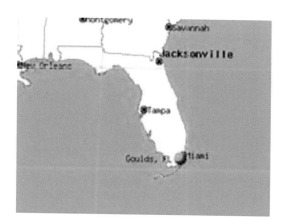

"For I know the plans I have for you," declares the LORD,
"plans to prosper you and not to harm you,
plans to give you a hope and a future."
—Jeremiah 29:11

Goulds is a town in Miami-Dade County Florida. A town of about three miles, it was named after Lyman Goulds and originally an old railroad town that had a rough population along the Old Dixie Highway. The bordering townships are South Miami Heights, Redland, Cutler Bay, Princeton and Quail Heights. Mainly poor black families live in Goulds. The Miami-Dade County continues to have a high foreign-born population today and this has grown since the 1970's and 1980's, due to Florida's high percentage of immigration from all over the world but especially Latin America. Cuba, Italy and Germany. Close to one million people in Florida were foreign born in 1980, with Miami-Dade County being a main hub for immigrants to settle over the last three decades. This is incredibly taxing on the area's economy, resources and size. In the 70s and 80s, it was the black population that dominated Goulds, however in 1970 over 1.2 million foreigners inhabited the land. In the early 1960s, many Cuban families migrated to South Florida and the Miami metro area during the 60s and 70s. Today , Latin American countries contribute to it being known as a city of immigrants. This has population increase has led to overcrowding in schools, high crime and draining of resources leading to poverty in certain areas.

Goulds was considered a ghetto in the 1970s and 1980's. Towns like Overtown, which were originally strong communities for black-owned businesses and black families before the 1960s became an area where black families were disbursed in the 70s and 80s. Liberty City, part of Miami-Dade County had almost historic race riots in the 1980s, with police killings of blacks, mistreatment of blacks and lack of opportunities for the black population living in Liberty City. Goulds is considered to be a part of the south of Miami-Dade and is considered a Miami ghetto, complete with housing projects which were a big part of making the ghettos, which existed because of extreme overcrowding of people. Migrant workers also were a significant part of the landscape for the Miami-Dade counties and they lived in extreme impoverished conditions. All of these factors made life extremely dangerous for a young Marriese of 5-12 years old, who was often running the streets by himself at an early age in Goulds and the neighboring communities.

Goulds was where this young boy would begin his journey in life. Born at Jackson Memorial Hospital in Miami, Marriese Alexander Jones, Sr. was born to Geraldine Jones, daughter of Solomon and Maggie Jones. Solomon and Maggie worked and raised a young family in southern Alabama and eventually settled in South Florida to raise a family that would grow to 17 children.

"For you formed my inward parts;
you knitted me together in my mother's womb.
I praise you because
I am fearfully and wonderfully made...
my frame was not hidden from you when I was made in
secret, intricately woven in the depths of the earth.
Your eyes saw my unformed substance;
in your book were written every one of them,
the days that were formed for me,
when as yet there were none of them."
—Psalm 139: 13-1

Introduction

To write of one's life, my life could be said it is like me living it twice, huh? Now that can be good and bad, hmm? Because to live it once for me may be enough, huh? But to live it twice? Recounting the whole story, huh? Now that can be a lot. That can be hard. But I have to tell it, hmm? I have to get it out, huh? For me, it's like I can't keep it in, huh? Huh? And I've always been that way. Yeah. I just say it. Sometimes that's good and sometimes that's bad, boy, it's got to be told, hmm?

I guess I started telling my story to the public in Walsenburg, Colorado where I was the guest speaker at an event for Colorado State University's **Walsenburg Action Institute-Hosted by the Colorado Food Policy** Network (<u>COFPN</u>) on October 12, 2015. I was with my good friend, Rusty Collins, and I had just graduated from my Family Leadership Training Institute (FLTI), class. Yeah, this is where I began telling my story about some tragedies in my life and the people were amazed, huh? They were so happy and so supportive of me, hmm? I thought, wow! They're lining up to see me and talk to me! They were crying and I wondered, *Why is everyone crying?* It was so crazy! I couldn't believe it! Those people wanted to hear my story, huh? See, God's going to make a way, hmm? One way or another, huh, God is going to make a way for the story to be told. Yeah man. They loved me, yeah. They loved me, I'm telling you.

So, I knew then, hmm, that the story had to be told, huh. Not for me, hmm? But for them, huh? For the people. They had to understand what it was like for me me and growing up in South Miami. They do not know what it is like for a black family. They don't understand what was like for our family and the daily struggles which was life for us. This book only skims the surface. The next book will be an in-depth account of my mother and my story and what she went through. They don't understand what it was like for me growing up in a place like that. and what I overcame from my childhood and then in life as an ex-felon. And also I don't say I'm African American. I am not African, huh? I have never been to Africa. I am a black man. A black man living in America. Huh? Huh? They have to understand, hmm, that we did what we had to survive. People have to know the story. Yeah, man. And it's going to take many books because the story can't be told completely and fully in one book, huh? There's too much! There is too much. But it is my life! But there is much to be shared, if one will listen, hmm? There is so much to be learned by the average person, huh, who didn't experience any, not even a tiny amount of what I went through and what I overcame. And to have what I have today? To be where I am today? That took a lot of hard work and focus, hmm?

I went to a college class last year. I became an honorary classmate at Denver Seminary of all places. Isn't God amazing? He had me go into this class and share a bit to the students on cultures and black culture. The students loved my presentation so much. They asked for me to come back at their final class of the year. They interviewed me for their papers. The first day I was telling them that I had wanted to go to college, huh? That this was my dream too, to get my college degree. But college for the black family of my day was not even a thought! It was not even a thought! We were just glad to eat. We were just glad that we made it, huh, that we were alive and not dead or in prison? Can you even relate? Can you even understand that I had dreams too to go to school and have opportunities? Can you even understand that opportunities in my day were just seen as crazy dreams? I mean those people would think boy you crazy! You crazy to think about college! But I wanted it, huh? Just like everyone else I thought about it, huh? Just because I grew up with a hard life doesn't mean I did not have the same desires as other kids my age. It just seemed like an impossibility, hmm? I finished high school in prison, huh? With my GED. That was my college, hmm? Prison.

So, this book isn't for the weak. It's not a feel-good story, huh? There's some stuff in here, man. There is some stuff. Because that's life! That is life. And it's real. And sometimes nobody wants to talk about the hard stuff, hmm? But I was suffering! I was suffering. I always knew I'd get out, but I didn't know how, huh? And in the black communities there is a rule that is unspoken. It is that what happens in the family stays in the family. We don't talk about any of it much. So, it's like this bubble that grows and gets bigger and bigger. That's how it was in my family too. And eventually the bubble bursts. For me it burst and I went on the streets of Miami and to prison.

So today, I am proud, huh? I am a proud black man, proud of all that I have accomplished and all that I have overcome. This here is my dream. And for where I came from and all I overcame? Working three jobs for thirteen years to make it through and get my restaurant and non-profit, that is an accomplishment, huh? To have a sound mind after all I went through and not be on medication or crazy, huh? And to be a leader investing in and building the young generation and developing other leaders, hmm? Now that is a miracle, huh? And it is all self-taught. I had to teach myself. I am self-taught in cooking, in business, in leadership, in counseling and in common sense. Because no one thought I would even live past a young age, huh? My family thought I would die, hmm? After what I overcame and what I was becoming, they thought I would surely die. But God had a different plan for me. God said, "Surely you will not die, but live and you shall surely LIVE." GLORY TO GOD.

So, come along with me, huh? Come along with me as I take you on a journey to my childhood and where I began, hmm? I won't tell the whole story now, but I will tell pieces of my memories and you will start to get a picture. So, come with me to Goulds, Florida and walk with me in the streets like I did as a five-year-old boy. See what you think, huh? Put yourself in my place. I'm gonna take you there now. I'm gonna take you back with me on this journey. Come along for the ride. And then I promise my next book will be a cookbook, huh? Yeah, I promise you that!

Part I

(1968-1980)

Memories of a Young Marriese

12 years

Chapter 1

My World of Tears

5 Year old Marriese cooking for his dad

"The LORD is my shepherd; I lack nothing."
—Psalms23:1

I cried every day.

Every day I cried. I was fixin' to answer him yellin for me, uncertain of what I done to get what was comin. I figured there would be a whooping as he called it. Still, I ain't much liking the idea and wanted to know the particulars, so I stepped down from my box by the stove where I had been standing for a long while, it seemed. He had told me earlier to fix him a plate and so that is what I done, but it was Sunday. And Sunday could mean a drinkin day. Fridays and Saturdays was meaning drinkin days for sure, but Mondays, Tuesdays, Wednesdays and Thursdays were mostly okay which meant that he was not drinkin. But Sunday, could mean either. Sometimes it meant it was the last day he would drink before he went off to work on Monday or it could mean not a day of drinkin. So, when he called me to come in after I had fixed his plate, I didn't know which Sunday it was. I didn't know neither when I had started fixin the plate but I figured I'd know soon enough. I didn't much like him on those drinkin days. He was so mean. He was as mean as a rattlesnake. So, I poked my head around the corner of the room and there he sat, high up on the edge of that chair of his that he sat in every day when he was yellin at me for this thing or another. Yep, he was sittin on his chair, with the plate on his lap and his mouth was in a tight line across his face. I saw a bottle of beer that was half gone on the table, so now I figured what was comin. He wasn't much lookin at me and for a minute I had figured maybe I'd get away clean. Now, I may have had a mind to walk to my room, but right then I heard him again say, "Come on", in his rough voice and it stopped me dead in my path. I could feel my body tensing up. So, I turned around fast as if to play that I had been the whole time comin over to him even though I ain't 'bout to be runnin for another beatin anytime soon and I'm sure he saw me tryin to get away. "What is this?" he asked me. Now, I may have been only five but I had enough sense to not be bad-mouthin my daddy, so I looked at the plate still in his hands and then looked at him. It seemed like a question that I shouldn't much answer, cause after all if he had looked at it, he'd surely seen what it is. I knew fo sho then he ain't right in his thinkin and this could only be bad for me, so still not lookin at him I quick was lookin back at his plate and I figured that 'cause he ain't eatin it, he must to want me instead to put up his plate. But then he said again, "What this is?" and now I was knowin he was tryin to be funny but not in a good way for me, no. I was thinkin to tell him it was his plate I had done just fixed so carefully for him, but I figured it best not to say nothin 'cause I knew he'd think that I was surely tryin to be disrespectful to him. Well, tears started to get in my eyes because I had really tried so hard for him tonight and I wanted him to like my cookin. I just stared at the plate and nervously counted all the items that he had told me to fix. It looked right to me and just then the plate took a tossin that made it fly through the air and his food that was on it went crashing onto the floor, adding a mess of beans, grits and fish to the carpet. I heard a gasp leave my body and I hit the ground quick so I can be cleanin up his mess. I figured then that he must'n much have cared for what I was fixin him for supper then and I tried to stop the tears from fallin on my cheeks but they just kept comin. I was sure what was 'bout to be happenin next and I very much wanted to get away but soon the expected came with his fist and it must have been gaining speed in the air 'cause it came smashing down on the side of my small head by my ear in a *whack, whack, whack* which knocked me so hard to the ground that I lay face down in the beans. The ringin in my ears was loud and for this reason I didn't like it when the whoppings hit my ears, 'cause they were very sensitive and they hurt me, but I just closed my eyes tight and got ready for more poundings to come from this man who was my dad. It was more the knowin that I done disappointed him again that made me the saddest. The hittin I had become used to it. Tears of mine started to fall and this I knew he was fixin to be angrier when he saw me crying. *Whack, whack, whack,* again this time the other side of my head went numb and I couldn't hear him. "Daddy, stop!" I yelled. Well, I was knowin he ain't fixin' to stop. I do remember more of *whack, whack, whack* again. *Whack, whack, whack.*

I suppose it was a particular night because I remember it well, but there was nothin so special 'bout it. I do recall however, that I lay awake in my small bed room after that happenin. I laid there for a long time and then when I ain't hear dad rustling around in the kitchen, I figured he must have fallen asleep again in his chair in front of the television. Fixin' to go to sleep myself, I buried my head into my pillow and sobbed. I very much was tired of this. Tired of worrying, tired of my head hurting and tired of crying. I didn't want to cry anymore, I just couldn't help it. I was so sad. I wanted my suffering to be gone. My heart hurt so much. No one cared that I was beat again tonight. No one loved me. No one. I knew that dad couldn't help but get mad at me. But I had tried hard today to fix his plate right, I ain't so good at hearing him 'cause the TV was always so loud. Maybe there was something wrong with my ears, I got to thinkin, 'cause I can't never hear dad and I forget things that he wants on his plate. But that's no reason to hit me, I heard myself saying.

When I fix dad's meals I am standing on my box so I can reach 'cause I'm not all tall enough to work the stove. I fix him good plates of fish, greens, cornbread, eggs, grits, potatoes, beans. But sometimes, when Dad drinks and shouts at me, I get it wrong. And he never repeats himself. I try to listen good so I don't miss anything and fix the very best plate for him, but when I can't hear it all, then he beats me, like tonight. It was a bad night and my the pain in my head just aint stopped.

I hurt all over but most of what hurt was my heart. I cried some more till my eyes were swollen shut but I figured I couldn't much see if I opened them anyway, so I kept them closed tight. I very much wanted to disappear. I prayed to God to let me go away. I figured God doesn't hear me or very much care, since he never let me slip out. I pulled the covers down around my waist and pulled my knees to my chest tight. My hands covered both my eyes, holding them because they were sore now. I was hot but the air was now on my uncovered skin from a breeze that was cool from my open window and that felt good. The hot and steamy house made me feel worse but I liked the breeze 'cause it made me sleep good. Slowly my sobs stopped and I must have drifted off to sleep 'cause I don't have any more memory of what happened next that night.

When I woke in the morning, the sun was fixin to rise but it was still sorta night outside my window. The cool night air was gone now and the heat of the morning was makin it's way across me and I wanted to take off, but I just lay there trying to figure what to do next. My eyes still were fat and swollen. Since I was not sure what the day was fixin to be, I didn't mind much to stay layin in my bed. *I ain't knowin if it will be a day of sadness again so why get up?* I was thinking. Some days, I would be fixin to go fishin or to Grandma's house and a little bit of happiness would be in me and make me jump right out of bed. This day however, I was feelin extra tired from the whooping the night before. My mind was thinking fast with thoughts of dad fixin to beat me again and then the sad thoughts filled my heart to know that I may be doin lots of cryin all day this day too. All that thinkin and cryin sure gave me a headache so bad that my head was a poundin.

I was small, with a head full of hair, and a playful smile although there were days that the heaviness seemed to overtake me, so that if you saw me you may wonder what could have happened to make me seem so sad. I had so much that was expected of me by my dad who wanted me to be more of a companion to him then to know that I was still a kid. All my entire childhood, no one cared much that I was young. No one had the mind to know I was only a boy, except maybe Grandmother. They stole that from me, making me to be grown. I remember that. Life was bad for as long as I can remember. I always did what they told me to do, but I wanted very much to be like all of the other kids. It was not that way for me, no it was not that way.

His name was Bill, my dad that is. Bill was a hard man. He was made of stone and he was raising me while Mama was away, which at times was a lot for me to understand in my mind. My mama was gone. She was working to support her siblings 'cause nobody cared for them. My dad was a good provider for me and Mama, but for whatever reason unknown to me as a five-year-old kid, all I knew was that Mama left me in the care of this man who beat me often if not always. He could never much control his temper and I just figured that my dad was feelin some kind of way about me 'cause he saw the beatings as fittin for me. He always said that he was doin what was best for me and I suppose maybe he saw it that way. He would tell me that he was teaching me independence, even if I was only a kid. I later wondered if he ever had any guilt he felt for his continued yellin and hittin me and I wondered if he bought me nice things because of that. So, I suppose my dad made a life for me the best he could done but his lack of patience and anger always seemed to get the best of him, especially when it came to me. I never was really sure what I done. I'm figurin that dad must have known that he was not a good father to me, but maybe he did not know about being a father. He wanted me to have the best and that he did and I sure never wanted for nothin in the way of things. I think he figured he knew how to give me the tough lessons that would help me live in a very hard and cruel world like Gould's and Miami. *Maybe he was just doin to me what his father had done to him*, I'm thinkin. *After all, what did he know about raising kids?* He might have well realized that none of this made it easier on me, but since he couldn't help it, he would just be harsh and not go changin. After all, he built manholes and oversaw a construction yard, so of course he was tough. I wonder if he knew he was wrong in hittin me so much, but it was too late to change him or me now. He would just make up for it by making sure I had things and money. What was love after all?

****

So, yeah I do vividly remember all the beatings and when they started, which was before I was five. My life as a child? Well, was it ought to be filled with pain and mistreatment, huh? After all, what could I have done in those five years that would have deserved that kind of disregard, to be doing that kind of wrongdoing to a youngster? Do kids live through this stuff? I didn't know because I didn't much know about things like that back then. I didn't even know at the time it was wrong, it just felt bad. How could I have done such wrong to anyone with only a few years of livin, huh? What do kids feel like when faced with such misconduct by adults? We can only guess most of the time. But I do recall and can speak on it now. I outlasted it, but I suppose I could have just as easily not. I was too young to think about dyin. I suppose I was too young to worry about tryin to live too. There were many more days and nights of hidden pain for me.

For much of my strugglin there was only quietness by me, yet the remembrances are strangely vivid for the mind of a child. Instead of the memories fadin and leavin gaping holes that one can't see, like in a fog that never clears after a hard rain, these times of darkness played like a constant movie in my mind, when I cared to think on them, that is. I can feel myself still as a child cryin many tears, like the heavy summer rains that go on for days. I can recall the tears as they would never end. I especially remember the love that was missin from my life from those who a child is to be loved by, a Mama and a Daddy. I can still feel the constant ache in my heart that pierced me all the time. My life was so hard as a little boy. Everythin weighed me down and a deep sadness covered me like a black blanket. I feel like my childhood was stolen from me. My childhood was taken from me because I had to grow up fast, endure so much and learn to fend for myself. I hurt. I hurt so bad and no one cared. No one even saw me. It was like I was invisible at times.

Some of the time felt too dried up and that one more tear couldn't squeeze out of my eyes. My chest hurt where my heart was quite often and this was mostly what brought the pain burstin out of me like a river. To remember everything, actually is a miracle I have been told. There were so many nights that I felt no love or care from any of them, feelin completely alone and hated by my family members, by my blood. But a few loved me so much and I could feel their love. Because of their love I was sometimes light, free and joyful. These times were waters of refreshment for me in a dry desert. So, it was very much not just one way or the other for me, but both. My life is much of this and that. Both hated and loved. I was both neglected and abused by those who were supposed to love me and yet loved by those who were not really called to have love for me like that. From as long as I can remember, there were struggles in and around my life and for a child of my age and size, I recall I didn't much care for that turmoil. I was a youngster in a war zone in a way. It was my own war and my battle was to survive. What makes the difference between those who outlast the mistreatment by adults and those who lay down? I guess I had a certain strength and determination to live and that was deep inside of me. I believed in God at a young age and as much as I didn't have love, my Grandmother was an example that love was true and existed. I saw others in our family had it and I wanted it too. I suppose that my longin for love at an early age would be great and even though I could not find it, I would love others deeply from the core of my being.

I found a man in the bushes.

In the bushes, I found a man. But I ain't yet to that part of the telling. I recall that I had jumped quick out of bed. I was happy not sad on this day 'cause I remembered that day was fixin to be a great day. The house was quiet that morning and that was unusual. Usually it was noisy with my father bangin around early, gettin ready for work. That day, I was goin to collect cans and bottles and go on to Grandma's house. I was yellin and hollerin and happy that no one was home but me. I got dressed very fast and was quite excited. I fixed myself a plate. I was thinkin, Dad is gone to work, and I ain't sad that he is gone, I am glad. He won't be tellin me what to do today. I can get ready by myself. I even washed my own diapers when I was little. Dad used to pour bleach in the toilet and I would have to rinse out my dirty diapers and clean them. I was two years old then, but I had to do it until I was four years old. But not now, I don't wear diapers. I am grown, I'm five years old now. Hurryin, I done took off out of the house for the way to Grandmother's and Granddad's. I figured, Dad won't be home till later, so, I was goin to stay late at Grandma's today! It was not Friday. It was not Saturday or Sunday neither so I ain't fixin' to get a beatin. It was Monday and so he ain't gonna hurt me today, I said to myself. I was thinkin that I had to be workin on my hustle and sell these bottles and cans and make money and then I can go to the store. I put my sandals on just like dad showed me and off I went. I wanted to get lots of bottles and cans from the bushes and garbage cans today, I thought. If I sold them I would get money! It's was a great idea to me! I was so happy, no dad to hit me on this day.

Runnin fast, I headed to the paths that cut from the street to Grandma's house. In Miami and Goulds, there are always shortcuts and paths and the best bottles and cans are in the bushes. The air was still hot and gettin more heavy with the mornin turnin into afternoon. Loud screechin bugs was everywhere and I was walkin quite a bit slower now. The wet air made me take off my shirt and wipe my eyes and nose. I was used to the way it was by my house. It was always fixin to be hot where I lived. Even worse was at my fishin hole but there I had the water. I liked my town I guess, or at least it was what I knew. I liked being outside, I felt free. I liked the sound of the bugs, too. I used to catch them at the fishin hole and put them on my string to get the fish. Bein alone was okay, I guess, some of the time. I kept goin on now, runnin even though I was hot. The bushes was high above my head most of the time, so I was thinkin I was hiding from the cars and the people. I liked being covered. Sometimes I would see people on the path but not today, it was just me today.

I was breathin hard now, cause I was runnin so fast. I wanted to hurry so I could get the cans and bottles before other folks. I had an old bag I found in the kitchen, it ain't too big, but it would do. The bushes was heavy with leaves it was sometimes hard for me to get a good look. I had to get my head in real far to be seein and look between the prickly branches. It was hard work. I didn't much like the searchin, but I was okay with the pickin of the cans and bottles. They were sure all sticky and bugs was mostly stuck to the tops where I guess they be wantin a drink but done ain't be gettin away. I ain't much care one way or not if they was there and they didn't give me no care neither. I stuck my head in real far into one of the bushes, makin sure to close my eyes real good on the way in so I ain't get poked by no stick and on the way out I seen the strangest thing I never done seen before. It was somethin really big. And although I ain't seen what it was, my feet they found it. I tripped right onto it. Catchin myself real good I stared straight at him. It looked like he had fallen but somehow I just was knowin that he neither had fallen in those thick bushes nor he was sleepin He was a big man and it scared me, 'cause I ain't thinkin I would find him in here when I was can huntin. Frightened but curious, I be squintin my eyes and bent down real close to him to me get a good look. That man was shot and looked to me to be bein dead. Now, I ain't never seen no dead man before and I'm ain't quite certain how I be knowin he was dead at all. But, I was seein blood all over the ground, so I was guessin he was dead. I just figured. Well, I started cryin or at least my eyes were waterin a lot and I run faster than ever to Grandma and Granddad's house but I ain't a bit scared. I was curious and I was gonna tell them what I seen. I heard some older kids talkin about dead folks and I know I had seen one too. But why then was I kinda cryin? I guess I just kept seein his eyes lookin down as if he was thinkin on somethin, but I knew from the way he was layin that he ain't much thinkin on nothin. *It was like he had been thrown out with the trash and that ain't much fun for a man to be layin that way*, I was thinkin. I kept runnin, and feelin my face, 'cause it felt hot. I was shakin and my tears now were wet on my cheeks. I ain't want to keep seein him in my mind, that was kind of scary. Panting and cryin, I ran all the way to Grandmother's house.

I was not scared now, 'cause dad taught me to be tough, but I never seen no dead body 'fore and it very much bothered me at that moment. Being dead may have been a thought for me back then, but it was I ain't sure sure why or what I be thinkin on it. If I think on it at all, it be that most folks had been knowin somebody who was dead, so I figured lots of people was dyin. And I very much wanted to live. When I ran through the door at Grandma's I was panting so hard and I told Grandma what I saw. Grandma just said, "Oh, it's going to be okay. It's going to be okay, Marriese." "I could be dead like that man", I shouted. "But you're not" Grandma said, "Why don't you come into the kitchen with me while I cook? Let's just forget about what you saw, it will be okay." Hugging me tight, Grandmother put her arm around me, her youngest grandson, and walked me into the kitchen with her to fix us a plate. Grandma always told me,

"Everything is going to be okay, everything is going to be ok." And I believed her, yes, I did. I believed that woman, my grandmother.

****

Yeah. I seen many dead bodies in those bushes, I did. I just stepped over them though. They was all dead. I ain't like it much, but I was not scared. I was tough, 'cause I was five years old. My dad told me all the bodies were 'cause the people ain't paid the other people no money. So, I set out to in life to never be with no money. Life was confusing for me, with all that I saw. I was always happy to be with Grandmother, tho' in her home. As a five-year-old kid I learned to be where I was, no matter how sad. I just knowin I had to keep goin. I had to be brave.

My first job at five years old

At five years old I had my first job. My dad figured I needed to get my first job. I suppose, 'cause I was old enough. Yes, if you asked me what I was doin at age five, I would say "cookin and workin." I worked at my uncles's bar. My job was to put the silverware and napkins on the tables.

I learned that if I wanted money, I must be workin. Now, I ain't understandin how this man was my uncle and I very much wanted to figure it out. I thought about it all the time. I had been knowin that my dad didn't much like my uncle much and he ain't no relative to the Jones' side, so I ain't understandin how he bein in my life. But, I ain't gonna question no one and was fixin to do what I was told.

Remembering my dad and my world at age eight

I remember at age eight, my dad and my world had made me tough. My dad was tough as hell and I suppose he was seein that I was tough too. He really did plan it. He would tell me that if he ever died, at least I'd be independent and strong. He was determined to beat it into me, I figure. I was such a loving kid that it was hard for me and I endured so much in my years of livin. Yet, I was becoming used to seein all kinds of things. I had to have guts and wisdom to survive the streets back then. I had to be very smart at age eight, just to live. Yeah, I had to worry about living or dying. That was my world. Many days I was caring for myself, runnin the streets. 'cause when my father wasn't messin with me, he was just gone leavin me alone to figure everything out on my own. So, by the time I was eight, I had been runnin the streets for three years already. I was tryin to be about my hustle always, even back then. At eight it was nothin to see pimps beating their prostitutes, drug deals, people killing people, shootings and stabbings. All the hard things of a world that you can imagine, I done seen and lived it as a kid, in Goulds, where I grew up. The biggest hurt in my heart though was still my deep pain. I wanted love from the ones who I was supposed to get it from first in life, my mother and father. That love from them just ain't in my world at eight. No, not at all. And the others in my family, my large extended family? Shoot, those people ain't care nothin 'bout me. No, not at all and I am not exaggerating. Not one bit. Living with the loss of my family's love or, for that matter, never really havin it was a great tragedy in my life that I had to have courage to survive every day.

My father was wealthy and we was better than most people I was knowin, even better than my siblings or uncle's family. My dad's construction company gave him good money, so that man bought me everythin. We had a good life that way, I guess, with the money. I suppose that was his way of makin up for how he beat me, but the money was neither good or bad for a kid who is gettin beat up all the time. I was taught then to like nice things mostly 'cause of him. My father was somewhat nice during the week, mostly, but I used to get all wore out from his annoyance and irritability with me, which always seems to land a fist on my body somewhere. To say that I hated him for hittin and beatin me so much, was the truth. It was the truth. I was the only one of my siblings that had to live with an abuser. I went to visit my brother and sister at my grandparent's house, and always wondered why they got to live there and I didn't. They were happy and I was so miserable! Out of all the kids, I was the only one in my situation. I was the only one that could not live with my grandparents and my family and be happy. I just ain't understandin it! Why was everyone else happy and loved? Why was I left out as not good enough and then beaten? I was different than the others, cast aside.

So, I was abused and it was my father was abusing me. I was not understandin back then why my father had such dislikin of me to be acting all crazy toward me, but I just took it. There were years of bein hit. Years. Quite often, I thought I might die. Sometimes I suppose I wanted to. I didn't know if I would be dead of a broken heart or a broken neck. I didn't know one day from the next when it came to my dad. For me it was normal. My dad abused me verbally, emotionally and physically. Some days I would feel sorry for myself and want to fight back. You know, that's a normal reaction. But I said nothin for many years...or rather on the outside I was saying nothin. But on the inside, I was screaming.

My tears became a huge waterfall that would want to drown me in sadness. Sometimes the sadness made me feel so shamed inside. No one else was being abused, yelled at or beaten and I wondered, why me, huh? This tormented my mind and my heart. Why did I had to live through that? I would be crying and wondering why my dad or my family could not see me and how good I was? Why was I not good enough for my father? I could not understand why I had to be hurt especially being so young. So, I suffered each day. I fought this battle daily on my own. I fought a battle he and no one else knew nothing about. Not even today.

So, I really felt no love from anyone outside of my Auntie, (who was my dad's sister), or my Grandmother. And I could not understand it, comin from a family that was so all about love, why I didn't even get the love from my mama? So, I just kept believin in my heart that I was not wanted by no one, that I was very much hated by my family members and figured I was not good for nothin. I tried to stay happy, but there was so much sadness in me. I knew that I would one day get out of there, I knew that things had to change, that I had to make my own way. At eight years old, I was so wise and I was already planning on how to do my own thing. I just had to find out how.

Lookin back, I can't believe I survived what I did. A lot for a kid and it wasn't over yet. I knew then that it would be a miracle to not only make it out of Goulds, but to survive it at all. My entire family thought I would not live to an old age or even to middle-age. And they told me that! Can you imagine hearing that spoken over your life from the time you were small? I was never scared, but sad a lot, yet I was determined to live. I was goin to get out and do great things, I knew that. I suppose I had to be going through some hard stuff cause that's what my life was, yeah.

To survive this was nothing short of a miracle. Just to survive. It is impossible to understand. My dad's story I will never know, but I did wonder if he understood what he was doing to me? I will never ask him. I suppose my anger toward him turned to a sort of weird understanding, but that wasn't fixin to happen for many years.

I remember my world without my mama

My world without my mama I remember would be longing for her so much as any kid would do. I had a special yearning for Mama that just didn't quit. I used to think, *why did she have to leave me with my dad?* Didn't she know that he abused me, my head hurt and I cried every day? Where was she when I needed her? During these long years, I believed that my mother did not want me. Can you imagine believing that your own mother never wanted you to be born? I couldn't understand why I was not wanted. I longed so much for a mom and when she would come around I would want her there forever because I loved her that much. That love never left me. I was just so hurt that she didn't want me enough to be there for me in my situation. It really does something to a kid to grow up believin that your mom didn't love you. That is terrible. And that's all I knew since I was two. I remember lookin for her, waiting for her, longin for her and hopin every day she would come for me and remove me from this man. That never happened. I very much wanted my mama around when all of the other kids had Mamas who gave the public appearances of liking their kids. Years of seeing my uncles have my grandmother as their mama made me want Mama all the more I needed her so bad but she was always stayed away.

There were years of not havin a mother around when all of the other kids had a mama. Years of seein my uncles have my grandmother and I was so ashamed of who I was because my mama did not want to be around me. I was so embarrassed and I could not make sense of it in my head, so I would think and think on it and I would cry every day. My heart hurt me to my core. I tried to stay happy, but there was a deep sadness in me. I can still feel how I was feelin back then and my sadness was there from as long as I can remember. Yet, God kept the deepest longin in my heart for Mama that was so great I ain't never been able to deny it. It never went away, it just got greater. I tried to fill it with other things but the ache for her never left. It was an indescribable pain. Cryin was a release and sometimes the only release I had. But I was so sick of cryin, too. To love her that much and to think she didn't love me or want me. I just ain't never understood it. But I learned more when I was about seven and it eased the pain a little. I would go with Mama whenever she came for me and wanted me to go with her, because at least we were together. Nothin, not anything can ever replace your mother. Nothin in my world could replace what I needed or wanted from my mama and no one else could make up for her. She was the one person I needed the most. So, Mama started to come around more and more when I was seven and she would take me to the bean field. I would pick beans with her all day somedays. I was happy when I went with Mama, cause at least I was able to be with her there. I would make about $7.00-$8.00 for my beans and I would give Mama $4.00 of it to help her. Mama would pick beans and okra all day until her fingers bled sometimes. I loved her so much. Life was hard for her. She had her first child, my brother, at age 12 so she always had was workin hard. As a kid, you just accept what your life is, you ain't know no better. I knew Mama had to work and make money, so I wanted to help her. She was in the streets back then. She was lost to me most times and 'cause I loved her I wanted to make it okay for her. I wanted to take care of her.

Mama told me herself about what was happenin to her. I suppose she felt that I was old enough to know the truth at seven. It ain't her fault, she was forced to do it. See, Mama had been molested at a young age and ain't ended the whole time I was a kid. She was bein pimped out like a prostitute during those years by someone who was stronger than her. I was livin with my dad. She did this to support her other kids and siblings. There was no other work for her Mama and she had to pay rent and take care of them. In the day, Mama would be at the bean field and at night, she be hustlin the men. Then I had to start collectin money from all the men for Mama. So, my other job was this one and I didn't like it so much. My mama suffered, yeah she did, but she was strong. I ain't never seen that lady cry. I used to not understand, but now I see what my mother went through. Yeah, so my job was to go pick up the money. I did this between being 8-12 years old. Can you imagine this as a job for an eight-year old? Well, I had to do it so I just did. I did not like going to pick up the money from the men and I grew up not likin men. Not until much later would God heal me of that. But from that time on though I learned to never trust a woman, that she would never be faithful. But the love for Mama never left me, no not one bit.

I guess I did blame Mama at times because she

left me with my dad from the time I was five and I was thinkin she chose everythin else over me. That affected me. All I knew was that she stayed away from me most times. As a kid growin up, these are the kinds of things that I had to figure out.

I would come to know later that my mama's stayin away was her way of lovin me. She was trying to protect me. Her burden was so heavy for her with her responsibilities. Mama did what she had to do to survive. I learned so much from my mother and I have the greatest respect for her. For many years I was mad at her. Then God showed me the truth. Geraldine Jones, my mother, is the bravest woman I know and my best friend. Watch for my next book as it will honor my mother and tell her incredible story. What a woman! Today we are so close and I take her on a trip for her birthday each year.

The things I saw on the paths

On the paths, I saw things. In Miami and the areas around Miami, there are paths everywhere, shortcuts. On these paths, there are a lot of things that happen. I used to take these paths by myself and I saw all kinds of stuff that affected me as a kid! That's where the drug dealers and dead bodies were, and I saw lots of them by age eight. It was nothin for someone to take your life in Miami. People just don't know. I saw pimps beating up their prostitutes. A lot of times I would just stand there and watch. They would see me and yell, "Go on"! I would sometimes run at them and yell for them to leave that lady alone! I know I saved a lot of those ladies from being killed. See, I knew what was going on at age eight. Probably even at five. Can you imagine seeing what I saw at that age? I saw it all. I was tough as a kid, yeah I was. I had to be.

Old Slick

"Old Slick" I remember. Life growing up in Miami was hard. We saw so much as just kids. I remember 'Old Slick." He was always cut and bleeding. That man was always cut, every weekend! That lady Helen, she cut Old Slick and he just kept going right back to her. That was one mean lady there boy. He just was always bleeding, laying on the sidewalk. He just kept going back. And she did this for years! Old Slick.

Pee-Wee

Pee-Wee. I remember Pee-Wee. Pee-Wee died, boy. That boy killed Pee-Wee. Beat him with a brick until he was dead. Yep, he killed him. Man, it was nothing for us to see dead bodies and people die in Miami. We'd just step over the dead bodies. Growing up in Miami was like nowhere else in the world. To even survive it was something.

When Mama was in trouble and God spoke to me clearly.

God spoke to me clearly when Mama was in trouble. It was God talking to me on that day, but it sounded like Mama's voice. I was in the third grade and I liked girls of course. There was a girl I liked in my class. This day I was going to a party, but it wasn't until later that night. The girl I liked was going to be there and she told me that she would sleep with me. I really, really wanted to go to this party. When night came and it was time to go to the party I was runnin down to the end of my yard by the street when I heard Mama's voice! But it was so weird because Mama wasn't screamin, she was talking softly. *But how could I hear her?* I thought, because I knew that I was too far away from the house to hear her! But I clearly heard her and she was saying, "Baby I need you." She sounded so worried and it sounded like she was cryin. Quick, I turned around and ran to find Mama in the bathroom bleedin all over the floor from between her legs! She was so weak she could not stand up. So that night I ran as fast as I could to my grandmother's house. My grandmother and granddad came quickly and took Mama to the hospital. They said Mama had a miscarriage and the doctor said Mama would have died there on the bathroom floor if I had not gotten to her. If I would had not listened to God talkin to me, my mama would have died. God told me to go to my Mama that night. Yes, he did.

"I will pass over you, no destructive plague will touch you."
—Exodus 12:13

Chapter 2

Fishing

Young Marriese fishing in the Catpoles

"

He who believes in Me, as the Scripture said, 'From innermost being will flow rivers of living water."

—John 7:38

When I was 7-8 years old, I would fish...

I would fish when I was 7-8 years old. It was something I did all while growin up. I loved to fish. It was the one place I would go and never cry. I was always happy there. I had no fishing pole but it was ok, 'cause I used a stick and then I use to pull strings from Grandma's rug. I would grab my stick and my string and I would take off. It was more like a mud hole, but I loved it.

Everyone used to laugh at me cause I pulled out the strings from the rug but I didn't care at all if they did. They didn't know how I needed to go fishin. I need to be there. Grandma always told those people to leave me alone. It was where I could hear God. He was there with me at my fishing hole.

****

Maggie Jones was my Grandmother and she was born in 1925 in Alabama. She married her soulmate "Boy" Jones, my Granddad Solomon Jones. During her life, she took great pride in her vocation as a laborer and housewife. My Grandmother was everything in my world. I was her favorite. I knew that. Boy, did she love me. Wow. My Grandmother gave me so much that I am today. She used to always say to me, "It's going to be okay." Those were her words to me. And I believed her and guess what, huh? It finally is. Today, everything is okay. But back then, wow! Well, I didn't know.

"But whoever drinks of the water that I will give him shall never thirst; but the water that I will give him will become in him a well of water springing up to eternal life."
—John 4:14

Chapter 3

Grandma's Kitchen

Maggie Lee Jones

*"A generous person will prosper;
whoever refreshes others will be refreshed."*

—Proverbs 11:25

Grandma's kitchen is my favorite place to be.

My favorite place to be is my grandma's kitchen. I ain't waitin no more. I jumped on my hot wheels and took off!! Grandma's house was only a few streets away. Jumpin off my bike fast now, I pushed it away from me and was runnin for the door. I was fixin to find Grandma and my cornbread! I ran into the kitchen. Well, there wasn't no cornbread on the counter and no Grandma! I was so mad and I was a hollerin, "Grandma! Where's the cornbread?" I still ain't seen Grandma, so I went to hollerin again, "Grandma! Grandma! Wheeere is the dammmn cornbread? !!!!" Just then Grandma came round the corner. Now Grandma wasn't very big I was thinkin, and by now I had figured she heard me 'cause she was lookin straight at me with that look in her eye, and I knew she was fixin to tell me somethin.

"Boy", Grandma said back with her finger in the air a waving it all over the place, "Now don't you go cussin like that!" My grandmother was tough too, uh huh, she don't like us kids comin in and yellin, no. Grandma walked calmly over to the canister where she carefully wrapped and hid a few special pieces of cornbread just for me, her favorite grandson.

Boy, did I love this woman. She raised me with Mama gone. My uncles were like my older brothers. Yeah, they all laughed at me. My grandmother and I spent many days in the kitchen together. My dad never wanted to take me to her house, so when he wasn't home I would go over. All the other kids would be outside playin basketball and sports, but I just wanted to be in the kitchen with her. It was a happy place for me. They used to make fun of me, but I didn't care. I learned to cook just like her. But that was my place. I loved it and I loved being with her.

****

My mind wanders to the laughter that often filled the rooms of Grandmother's house. It was always flooded with cousins and uncles and aunts runnin in and out. Oh, how I loved being with my grandmother in the kitchen cookin and spendin time with her! It was my place with Grandma. I think of grandmother and her home often. Oh, how I loved her cornbread especially.

The time I spent in the kitchen with Grandma was so special to me. All of that time with her would birth in me a love of cooking so great that I knew that was the place I most loved to be. It was the place where I could think and figure things out, a place where I could make some sense of my world, 'cause that is where I could have calm and peace back then, in Grandma's kitchen. It was safe there. And so goes part of my story and the tale of a great love between Grandmother Maggie Jones and me, her grandson Marriese. A future chef was born, and a great man of passion and heart would be cultivated here, in those same slums of Goulds.

My grandmother, well she was one of God's greatest provisions for my life ever. Actually, for all of us. For me, I made it through and her love was foundational for my life. She saved my life in so many ways. It was one truth I kept coming back to. That lady loved us like no one else in the world and it was unconditional. Her love changed my world. Today, I love like she loved. I feel like she lives on through me.

"So whether you eat or drink or whatever you do,
do it all for the glory of God."
—1 Corinthians 10:31

Chapter 4

The Shoes

"My command is this:
Love each other as I have loved you."
—John 15:12

Grandma was always giving things to strangers.

To strangers Grandma was always giving things. When people came into Grandmother's house, she would wash their clothes, let them eat at the kitchen table and talk to them. Then Grandma would pack them food to take with them. Sometimes she would give them things of hers! She was always wantin people to have stuff when they left her house. There were lots of people comin to visit Grandma. They would tell her they love her, too.

One night I was goin out with my friends, to have a good time and go dancing! I loved to dance! I left my new shoes by the door before I was gone. When I got up in the mornin, I went to get my shoes, but I ain't find them anywhere. You know, dad always made sure we had nice stuff. Man, I looked everywhere for my shoes! They were nowhere! "Grandma", I was yellin. "Grandma, where my shoes at? I can't find them no where!"

Grandma came into the room and said, "I gave them away last night."

"You did what?" I screamed and started to fuss cause I was so mad at her.

Grandma just looked at me. She was so tiny but when she looked at me, I couldn't speak. "He was homeless and he had no shoes", she said, "You have lots of shoes Marriese," she continued.

"But they were brand new Grandma!" I yelled. Grandma just stared at me. I was so mad at her!

Maggie Jones was real. She was loving and the matriarch of our family and she led by example. This is how I am today. I remember, when some of my Grandmother's kids were on crack and in the streets, she would pick them up, take them home, wash their clothes, feed them and get them cleaned up, give them money and take them back to the streets. What unconditional love! Can you even imagine? If you came to Grandmother's house, you was never going to leave hungry or empty handed. She was gonna wash your clothes, feed you and give you somethin to take with you. That was Grandmother Maggie Jones. This is what everyone remembers about her. At Grandmother's funeral people came from all over to tell us stories about Miss Maggie Jones! She left a legacy of love to the world, yes, she did. I began to celebrate her birthday at the restaurant so that others know where I learned to love people to the way I do.

My Grandmother especially loved my mother. That was my Mama's best friend. During the years that Mama and I were not close, my grandmother always wanted me to go see my mother. I got to spend a few days with Grandmother before her death. She knew I was there. Today my mama is my best friend. I call her every morning. I guess I took the place of my grandmother in my mama's life. Isn't that amazing? I know that my grandmother would be so proud of the restaurant, but she would be even happier to see how Mama and I are today.

Grandmother lived by a code of love. Great was her love. She stayed with my granddad and even after he died, he remained the only man in her life up until she died in 2015. One time, she did leave and go to her friend's house for a while, but my granddad went and got her. She never left again. Her love started with loving my granddad and by being devoted to him, then to her 17 kids and grandkids and great-grandchildren. This was her family and she was going to love them no matter what. She knew each of her 47 grandchildren, 111 great-grandchildren and 99 great-grandchildren by name.

"Carry each other's burdens,
and in this way you will fulfill the law of Christ."
—Galatians 6:2

Chapter 5

A Night Like No Other

This night among all other nights shattered my world.

"He heals the brokenhearted and binds up their wounds."
—Psalm 147:3

I was 12 that day...

On that day, I was 12. Mike, my uncle was only a few years older than me, and he was my best friend. It was dark outside and Mike had me sittin on the handle bars, holdin onto me with one hand and I suppose steering the bike with the other. I ain't much remembering that part. But, I know we were ridin. And for a long time, we were ridin. Up and down streets, curbs, across driveways and grass, going fast. I could hear him panting as he tried to gain speed. I could hear him behind me breathin heavy. I was still cryin. The air against my wet cheeks made my face feel cold. Mike was riding me now on his bike and we was going fast. It was dark and I was freezing. I didn't know where we were goin. I guess it didn't much matter.

My memory is clear even now of that single moment. I looked at Mama. She wasn't lookin at me but she was lookin away. Mama just stood there with the gun in her hand saying nothing. I was just starin at Mama. Then I stared at my dad motionless on the floor.

I remember there was shots. They was so loud. I knew what they was, 'cause I had done heard them so many times growin up. And then silence...at least for a minute. Then screamin and cryin. People were runnin everywhere. I just froze. I couldn't move. It was my birthday, It was my special day. I was just standin there over the body of my dad when the paramedics moved over to take my Auntie in the ambulance. She had an asthma attack and almost died. They just left the body of my dad on the floor in the kitchen. I knew that meant people were dead when they just left you there. Uncle Mike was saying "Marriese, come on we got to get out of here." I told him, "No, I ain't goin nowhere, I'm stayin here." I didn't want to leave! "Come on", he said, "the police are comin." I looked at my dad on the kitchen floor. For some reason thought I should stay there with him. I was just feelin I ain't suppose to be leavin him. So, there I stood and just stared at him, on the ground. But, then I did it. I left my dad on the kitchen floor.Mike put e on his handle bars of his bike and we started to ride. He rode me all the way across the streets of Miami that night. Yeah, he did.

What was happening? What just happened? I was so confused. I think we were both shakin, Mike and me. At least I was. I know I was cryin. I can still hear myself saying, "He's dead, he's dead" I kept sayin over and over again through the night air. "It's going to be okay, it's going to be okay Marriese," Mike yelled back to me. I ain't see how. In my mind, I kept seein the vision over and over again in my mind. I saw it. I saw it. Dad was going after Mama. But before then, everything of my day was so perfect.

****

I remember that day, I was turnin twelve. I woke up fast! Not like the other days when I ain't get out of bed 'cause I was sleepy! No. Not on that day! That day was special! That was my big day! It was my 12th birthday and Mama was going to throw a big party. Mama always had the best parties and since she was home and celebrating for me, I was so happy. It was a day I had been waitin for, dreamin of. So, I woke up that mornin with excitement! October 1st. I had to wait though 'cause the party ain't be fixen to be ready until later! This was gonna be the best day, I remember thinkin! I was going fishin at my fishing hole that day. I wanted to celebrate the entire day! I headed over to Grandma's house but I had a real fishin pole this time, yeah. Dad got me one last year. You know he was hard on me. He still beat me all the time. I swear he was tryin to make me a man by beatin it into me! But I was a man. I was 12 on that special day of mine. So, I got my fishin pole and I took off! That day I had been lookin forward to, as much as any kid who was excited about their birthday. I had even put on one of my new watches that Dad got me. I'm was not thinkin of anything bad that day.

Dad sure did make it that I had nice things. I hated him 'cause he hit me so much and the beatings were all the time, but I ain't been thinkin 'bout that today. I was only happy. Nothin was going to ruin my birthday! Well the party started around four o'clock in the afternoon. Everyone was comin and Mama was still in the kitchen cookin. All of us kids were runnin around and havin fun. The food was startin to smell real good. My cousins and uncles and everyone loved to come over for Mama's cookin. We all did. I was so happy because Mama was there. My whole family was together for my birthday and I was being celebrated! It felt so great! I loved it! Grandma and Granddad were there too. My dad was the only one who was not there yet, but I didn't much care about that. I was my day and I was a celebrity! Ain't no one gonna make fun of me on that day! My party was perfect.

Well, when my dad finally showed up, He was not alone, which I knew Mama wasn't gonna much care for. It is kinda weird because I had never seen dad ever with anyone but Mama. I knew that Mama was gone a lot but dad still never had no woman ever besides Mama. Well, dad was there at my party but he was with a Filipino woman. I had never seen her before then and Mama was not happy at all and made that lady leave. I remember that made my dad very angry. They started to argue and I had very much wished that they wouldn't argue at my party. We were all havin fun. It was true that just last week dad threatened Mama with a knife. Yep, a big one, came right at her with it swinging in the air. Came right to her, I'm telling ya. Well, he was doin it again. Yep, he was drinkin and yellin and grabbed that big knife and I just watched him swingin it at Mama again. Now, Mama was afraid of no one so I knew Mama would fight back but I didn't know how. Dad was turnin into that other man again like he did when he whooped me, drinkin and yellin. I very much wanted them to stop yellin so much at my party. They were gonna ruin it. But I ain't much thinking 'bout telling my dad to stop and just then Mama reached right up in that cupboard above her head and grabbed that gun and started shootin. She had that gun and just started shootin, yeah. There were us kids runnin and screamin and gettin out of the way. Mama had shot that man. Yeah, she did. Yeah, she sure did. My mother shot my father that day, on my 12th birthday at my party. He died. That's the way I remember it on that day. That's my memory of my birthday.

****

What started out as the happiest day for me in a long time, a party filled with food and cake, fun and family turned into screams and bullets flyin and my father dead on the kitchen floor, shot to death. My parents now would both be gone... in an instant. What was I supposed to do? Who would take care of me? Where would my home be? What would my life be now? So confusin. So many thoughts racing through my head. I had no answers. I had nothin. And I would soon find out again just how little control I had over my world. I didn't much like birthdays after that and no one much cared if it bothered me or not. They just moved on with their lives, never much talkin bout it one way or nother. For me, I ain't like birthdays no more and I ain't celebrating them for a long time after that, no. I didn't talk about this much to anyone, at least not anyone who was a stranger and everyone in my family already knew why, so I never got it out. I always remembered it though. The movie in my mind never erased like it does for some people. For me, I see it and remember it all. I just pushed it down.

"For I am the LORD your God who take hold of your right hand and says to you, Do not fear; I will help you."
—Isaiah 41:13

Chapter 6

Shattered

Trying to make sense of my life

"So do not fear, for I am with you;
do not be dismayed, for I am your God.
I will strengthen you and help you;
I will uphold you with my righteous right hand."
—Isaiah 41:10

He was my father. He is gone at age 12.

He is gone at age 12. He was my father. The police arrested Mama but my Granddad got her out that night on self-defense. So, Mama was okay that way but she went to the streets after that and life was hard for us. I had to try to figure everythin out. About my dad. Well, I loved him and I hated him. On the one hand, it was just like him, to make problems. It seemed that nothin could ever go along peacefully, he always had to "mess everythin up." How many times had I tried to anticipate the outbursts and the yellin. Maybe I should be tougher now, I thought…after all my father was tough as hell. It always felt as if I was trying to make him not get angry or upset. Sometimes it was no use, his anger came out and no one could reason with him. He would not listen.

I had cried every day. EVERYDAY. EVERYDAY of my life. Many times, I thought, *how could so many tears had come out of one kid?* In a way, it didn't surprise me that he went after Mama with that butcher knife again. After all, he had done it the week before. Wasn't it just like him to do it on my birthday though? He always picked the worst times! No one could control him. How I wished sometimes that I had been bigger or stronger, so I could've stopped him. "One day," I thought, "I will be big and no one, I mean no one will ever hurt me or anyone I love again."

I hated him yet I loved him at the same time. After all, he was my dad! Ain't I supposed to love my family? These thoughts were so confusing. I tried to figure it out so many times that my head hurt. My dad had taught me many things. He taught me to drive! He bought me a car at 11! He was my nightmare and my hero. It was so confusing. I had to make this all make sense but it didn't. Where was God? Was he with me? I wanted my dad to love me. I wanted him to see how great I was. Did he? My head continued to have all of these confusing thoughts and I had to figure them all out on my own. They were overwhelming my mind. I know that my dad loved me. At least I am pretty sure he did. I don't know that he ever really liked me as a person though. Yet he would be actin so out of control and angry at nothin. I had no control over when he got angry. I had no control.

I hate not havin control. He hurt me, but I loved him. So, I ain't likin surprises no more neither. He surprised me with his anger all the time. He said such mean things. Ain't it just like him to have surprised us all this way? Why did he have to go and do that? Well, that time he may have done it. Mama had no choice. It was either him or her. I ain't believin he was gone. I could not believe it. What was I supposed to do now? I would shut it out. I would push it way down. No one was ever gonna hurt me again. I was angry, but at who? I was angry at God, at Mama, at myself. Maybe I should have been better. Maybe I should have tried harder to make him not mad. Maybe I should have been better than he wouldn't have gotten so mad always. Maybe...

"The LORD is near to those who have a broken heart, and saves such as have a contrite spirit.
—Psalms 34:18

Clean
by Natalie Grant

I see shattered
You see whole
I see broken

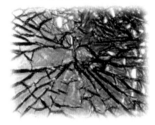

But You see beautiful
And You're helping me
To believe
You're restoring me
Piece by piece
There's nothing too dirty
That You can't make worthy
You wash me in mercy
I am clean
There's nothing too dirty
That You can't make worthy
You wash me in mercy
I am clean
What was dead now
Lives again
My heart's beating

Beating inside my chest
Oh I'm coming alive with joy and destiny
Ohhh
Cause You're restoring me
Piece by piece
Ohhh
There's nothing too dirty
That You can't make worthy
You wash me in mercy
I am clean

Oh yeah, oh yeah
There's nothing too dirty
That You can't make worthy
You wash me in mercy
I am clean
Washed in the blood of your sacrifice
Your blood flowed red and made me white
My dirty rags are purified
I am clean
Washed in the blood of your sacrifice
Your blood flowed red and made me white
My dirty rags are purified
I am clean
Oh yeah, oh yeah

Washed in the blood of your sacrifice
Your blood flowed red and made me white
My dirty rags are purified
I am clean
I am clean
I am clean
Oh You made me clean

"Heal me LORD and I will be healed;
save me and I will be saved."
—Jeremiah 17:14

Part I
(1968-1980)

Reflections by Marriese On My Childhood

12 Years

Chapter 7

A Broken Heart

My broken heart as a boy

"The thief comes only to steal and kill and destroy;
I come that they may have life,
and that they may have it to the full."

—John 10:10

I survived the abuse.

The abuse I survived. My abuse was now over. Yet, it still affected me so much. Everyone is different and everyone's situation is different. Many, many times I wanted to disappear. To get out of there. I always knew I would get out, one day. Everyone thought I would die and not live to an old age. But I got outta there. One way or another, I got out. I suppose I could have been dead of a broken heart or a broken neck. As a kid, huh, this was my life until I was 12. For me, my abuse was verbal and physical by my dad and emotional abandonment by Mama. I started out my life as a little boy believing that I was unwanted and unloved by my own mother and family. And that my dad didn't like me. Isn't that terrible? All of this was rejection of me to my core and that hurt me so much, man. This is what I grew up believing.

As a boy, I was just happy that my dad was not at home. Most days I would be home by myself, yeah. On the days he would beat me, sometimes I would want to fight back. You know? I was being whooped and beat all the time! But no one would help me or say nothin bout it to nobody. Whenever I could go to my grandmother's house it was great, but when my dad was fixen to be drinkin, I knew a whooping would be comin for sure. I ain't know for what but I sure know it be comin. I was never afraid of him though or of no one. I just hated him for whooping me so much. I hated him and loved him. I suppose he was trying to make me into a man the way he thought I should be. But I was a sensitive little boy and it affected me so much.

So, I would cry alone in my bed or other places every day. I was always wonderin why my dad and mama or my family could not see how good I was. Why was I sufferin so much? I was the only one in my family sufferin like this. I know that my father loved me, but it was a constant struggle cause I felt like I was not good enough for my dad or my mama. Maybe a part of me was dyin a little each day. Today, you will rarely see me cry. The real damage is always done on the inside. On the inside, I was screamin if anyone cared to notice. The waterfall of my tears was always building up. I had such great sorrow and pain. I did not celebrate my birthdays for so many years after the tragedy. I wanted nothin to do with birthdays as you can imagine. And no one in my family cared about that though. No one cared what I was goin through. The tragedy ruined so much for me.

After my 12th birthday, I moved to Orlando to live with my uncle Papa, that I respected so much. This was Uncle Leroy Jones and he was the oldest of my grandma's kids. Yeah, he took me in. I told that man everythin. He became the father I needed at the time. So, although I was runnin the streets right after the tragedy, I ended up goin to Orlando to live with Papa for a while. That was a blessing, caus I was runnin and searchin for something but I ain't know what. After my dad was killed, Mama was tryin everythin to support us and she had gone into the streets. It was a hard time for us. Memories of the abuse from my dad were battles I fought every day iin my head. I suppose I had some PTSD if yoiu want to call it something. These were battles no one knew nothin about. Not even today. I'm very private. To survive this was nothin short of a miracle. Just to survive! And I fought daily to survive. It was the hardest fight of my life. Man, those were some hard thoughts there, tryin to figure everythin out. Those thoughts haunted me till I was grown, until and I forced them all down and covered them with with anger. And I was so angry for so long. I had such resentment for my mother for abandoning me in that situation with my dad. I just ain't never understood her reasoning, 'cause I never knew the depth of what she went through, and wasn't fixen to know until later. That woman went through her own hell. Yeah, that lady was thinkin of me the whole time and loved me so much. I just never knew.

So, that bubble that that I mentioned that no one talked about was gettin ready to burst for me and it just kept growin and gettin bigger every day. There were so many parts of my bubble that were confusin to me as a young boy. I just ain't figured things out in my life until I became free of it and could look back and reflect. Like when my dad took me to my uncle's bar to work instead of grandma's house. I ain't never figured out how he was my uncle. I mean, how was this man in my life and a part of my world? My dad and my uncle never spoke much or got along, so why was he there? Things like that bothered me and I thought on them all the time until my head hurt so bad.

I remember that it took Mama forever to make the time to take me to the doctor when I was in constant pain for my head for so long. I was so mad at Mama about that. I just could not understand why she let me suffer for so long. When I was telling you that my head hurt, I mean it hurt! The doctors never did find anythin. Maybe the hurtin was 'cause my life was so crazy. I mean, there were so many things that were confusing to me and I had no one to help me neither.

When I think of how long I suffered in those days, I wonder how I survived it to be a teen. I will never know the answers to the questions I have for my abusive father. But I suppose I don't need to have those answers, because it was over and it ain't much matter. I just had to keep it movin. I had to keep my hustle up. I had to make sense of it on my own. In my childhood, I had no control of what was goin on in my world. But I was about to get control. I left Goulds, I made the decision and I left. I took the control. Boy, what I went through as a kid and the tragedy, no one will ever know. I had overcome so much. I overcame so much! I survived. Yeah, man.

So, my life is a story of conflict. I was happy he was gone, yet sad 'cause he was my dad. I loved Mama, but I was angry with her. I was abused, but I was taken care of. I was loved, but I felt hated. I wanted to stay, but I wanted to run. I wanted to trust, but I trusted no one. Who could make sense of my world? I needed to get away and get on my own. That should make it better, right? So, it was decided. I would set out, to take matters into my own hands. I knew that God had been with me the whole time I was little, but I was still gonna do it my way. s a kid, I was knowin He was with me when I was at the fishin hole and when I cried in my bed. God taught me when I was young how to hear Him and His voice, especially the time Mama had the miscarriage. I knew God was real and I ain't never doubted God speakin to me. But, it would still take some time before I gave up doing things my way. I knew God was with me, in all of it, all the time.

Maybe one day, I can write my story with some sort of understandin, 'cause only I will know that there was more to my story and more to uncover there then I knew back then as a kid. Maybe one day, God will give me a knowledge that not only was I being shaped for my life story and perfected in the image of the living God, saved by God and trained for His army, but I can one day understand the long threads of abuse and help others who are abused to move past their pain and into their glory when they can finally understand that it has nothing to do with them and who they are.

Maybe one day I can help others heal from their personal traumas and help them move from being victims to claiming their victories, realizing that that there is hope on the other side and only God has the power to heal it all. Maybe one day I can help others to see that, along the way, God was indeed weaving my story of courage and giving me a calling despite my story. Maybe one day I can help others to forgive their abuser so they may move on to a life of freedom in Jesus. Maybe one day I can give hope to those that feel hopeless because I could have lived a hopeless life, but I chose to help others

Maybe one day I can help lift others' shame because I too could have ended up living in shame from feeling unloved and treated so horribly, but God became my truth instead of man. Maybe one day I too can understand someone else's days and nights of endless tears because I too cried endlessly. I can understand how someone can feel what it is like to try so hard to do everything right, but it was no use because nothin was ever good enough for my dad. I felt that to a deep level. I lived it for 12 years. Yeah man, I can feel the people's pain.

Maybe one day, through my story, others can see and find the courage to survive their stories and can see themselves as not weak, but strong for just having lived through it. Maybe one day I will let you in far enough to see the depth of my pain, and then, yes then, I can write my story and encourage you one day to write yours.

"The LORD is close to the brokenhearted,
and saves who are crushed in spirit."
—Psalms 34:18

Part II
1980-1992

Memories of Marriese's Teen Years

12 Years

Chapter 8

Anger

I fought everybody

"Oh Lord, you hear the desire of the afflicted;
you encourage them and you listen to their cry;
defending the fatherless and the oppressed,
so that mere earthly mortals will never again strike terror."
—Psalm 10:17-18

I headed to the streets of Miami. At thirteen I was on my own.

At thirteen, I was on my own and headed to the streets of Miami. Looking back, I felt like the pain of mine would never quit in Goulds. I always knew I would leave and get out one day, but I never really knew how. I just knew it would happen. After my dad died, I left home and started to run the streets of Miami. Mama came from Baltimore and took me back with her. She married this man who spent my money and then had me breaking in houses with him to support his whores and his habits. So, I used to break in people houses and give Mama some of the money. I hated that man and my best friend gave me a gun and I said, I'm going to kill him", but instead I beat that nigga to sleep. He acted like he didn't tell Mama but he did. That's when I ran away again and stopped talking to Mom. Grandma said to just tell somebody where I was and she sent me to take care of my Uncle Leroy (Papa) when he had surgery on his knee, so that's how I got there, to Papa's house. Since he lived in Orlando I signed up for school there. My uncle was my hero. Uncle Leroy was the richest of all my Grandmother's kids and his house taught me love and how to be a man of God and family man. He was my hero and he loved me so much that he wanted one of his son's to be me...he was the one who I went to and told everything, just like Grandma told me to. After all of it, including the death of my dad, I was angry at everyone and I took it out on kids at school by beating everyone up there and on the streets if they crossed me. People were afraid of me. I was like a time bomb ready to explode, but no one knew when.

I met my real father

My real father I met. That's right, you heard me. So here are the details. Before I left Goulds, I met him. So, the man who I believed was my dad for all those years, the one that grieved me because I loved him and hated him all at the same time, not understanding why he beat me, yep well only after he died did I find out he was not my biological father. Try to now imagine a 12-year old that just survived a huge trauma having to wrestle with this as well. Do you remember my uncle's bar? Do you remember how my dad took me there to work and I could not figure out why this "uncle" was in my life? Yep, well you guessed it. My uncle was my biological father's brother. I had known my biological father all these years but never knew who he was. He had other kids but he never wanted me to be known, so I was kind of "hidden." I just accepted it because what else was I to do? So, I believed my mother did not want me and now I had a father that was not wanting to claim me. My biological father was an entrepreneur and business owner, too. He ran the bar. They were all smart and wealthy, my dad, my biological father and Granddad. They were all hard workers just like I am. My biological father was very mean according to Mama but I know later that he was proud of me. I look just like him. I actually took care of him right before he died. God allowed me that time to care for him. I knew he loved me so I am at peace now, but it was like adding gasoline to a raging fire burning within me at 12 years old. After all, how much can one kid take? I was just a mere child when my life had taken on many elements of an adult. I was maybe five or six at the most. But, I was determined to live and do it my way.

Back in Goulds today, many are still there and yet just as many have moved out. It actually is a small area, yet to a five-year old boy, it was my world. It was a world that was large enough to keep me swallowed up in it. I didn't know any better. I didn't know that people do not get shot and die young. I didn't know that selling drugs was not a normal job. I just didn't know. You see, that was my world and I would be trapped in it until I was 13 years old, with the good and the bad. Yet I was a fighter. I fought for my life back then and soon I would be a fighter on the streets of Miami

"Do not conform to the pattern of this world,
but be transformed by the renewing of your mind.
Then you will be able to test and approve what God's will
is---his good, pleasing and perfect will."

—Romans 12:2

Chapter 9

Locked Up

The young Marriese behind bars at 17

"He lifted me out of the slimy pit,
out of the mud and the mire;
he set my feet on a rock
and gave me a firm place to stand.
He put a new song in my mouth,
a hymn of praise to our God.
Many will see and fear the LORD
and put their trust in him."

—Psalm 40:2-3

I was arrested for armed robbery as a teen.

As a teen, I was arrested for armed robbery. I had actually robbed a police gun shop. I was fifteen. This did not look good. Considering where I came from and the life I had endured that far, it was not a far stretch for my future, I mean, you may have even predicted that I would end up locked up. I was a thug. They dragged the sentencing out until I was seventeen and I was able to go to school while I was waiting. They wanted to try me as an adult. Then, one day they came to get me while I was in school. They took me and I was free no more.

My family used to always tell me that I would end up dead or in prison. Be careful the words that you speak or let others speak over your life. God had the final say in my future, but the words we speak are powerful, hmm. So, I went to prison during my teen years. I was given thirty-seven months, but I escaped during a work-release program, so they caught me and my sentence turned into forty-four months. Prison is where God saved me from the life I was living on the streets of Miami. I became an honor inmate during my time there. I was elevated by the staff and guards. I used to give tours to school groups and talk to them about prison and obedience. God really elevated me in prison and I had so much favor. I always had favor in my life, even though it was sometimes hard to see. Isn't that just like Joseph when he was in prison? God elevated him and he gained favor with the guards. That is exactly what happened to me. Exactly. God gave me favor! He brought me to a place to stop what I was doing and showed me extreme favor!

I wanted to get married right away after I got out of prison. But I had a complex when I got out. Even though I was a model inmate, I was more bitter than when I went in. The system does that to you. No one cared about what I was going through or what I had gone through at home that 'caused me to get to be how

I was. They just locked me up. I was not rehabilitated in any way by being in prison. They call prison a "correctional system", but it corrects nothing! They isolate you and treat you as if you are not even human. That didn't do anything to help a teen who had been abused and traumatized as a kid. On top of that, when you are locked up, you get out and find out that you have 'lost' people. They died while you were in there and you have no one to care or help you grieve about the losses. People think inmates deserve what they get and maybe they do to a certain extent, but what about understanding why we are there? So many of us had our choices taken away when we were little or helpless. I had so much love in my heart as a child and I was beat down so much, to the point that nothing was left. Although I was an honor inmate and tried all I could, I was still hurting.

So, here is how I met my first wife, the mother of three of my children. My grandmother was moving to the projects in 1975 and this beautiful girl was moving out same day I was moving in. As soon as I saw her, I fell in love with her. And I told my grandmother, "Grandma come here, come here!"

"What Baby? " She asked.

I said, "Look at that girl! I'm going to marry her and she is who I'm going to have my children with." She was so pure, beautiful, and clean. I never wanted a bad girl for my wife. They left and then came back, and she walked in on my fourth grade class from Carolina.

When I got out of prison that girl saw my cousin and we connected right back. She did not tell me about her personal life then, but I didn't care. 'cause when I got out, I married her. I had seen her in the fourth grade and when I got out, I married her. I became an instant father to her two children. So here I was, out of prison and now a husband and a father. I always was sensitive and loved people deeply since I was a little boy, but I was so hurt from my past and had not dealt with anything that I was still suffering from, that not too long after I was out, I went back to prison for driving with a suspended license. That time I know that I went there for the guards. This is what happened. God told me that I was going to get out of prison and to get ready to go, so I packed up my stuff and went to the guards and arranged for all my stuff to be shipped home! The guards couldn't believe it! "Jones", they taunted, "You ARE crazy! You're not going home and we have too many other inmates who are getting out to deal with your stuff! Take it back to your cell and unpack."

I told them again with bold confidence. I said, "I am getting out, now ship my stuff!" For some reason, they listened to me! They sent it all home. Then, three days before the deadline for my sentence to be given, the notice was given to the staff that my charge was invalid and not legal. There was an inappropriate ruling of the law. I was sent home! God, literally shook the jail and the gates opened! God is so amazing! God got me out of there just like he told me! Those guards couldn't believe it. They could not believe what they saw.

One guard said, "Jones, go be with your wife and baby." My wife was in the hospital at the time having our baby. God got me out. I'm telling you, God has had favor on my life since I was a little boy. I am favored of God. My life has been hard, but favorable. It's been hard, but it's been favorable! The guards and inmates shouted at me, "You'll be back!"

"You're right, I said, "But on the other side to minister." They laughed at me, but in 2010 I did prison ministry at the Adams County Detention Facility, in Colorado. In 2016, I went to speak to the inmates at the Prison Entrepreneurship Program (PEP), in Houston, after I became a Texas Criminal Justice Volunteer.

Now although you may think that my path was clear from this point forward, it was not. I left prison to be with my new baby and wife but I would slip back into the drug scene to make money for my family. I was not able to get a job being an ex-felon, so how else could I support them. So, there was a long stretch of yet another detour ahead.

"And suddenly there was a violent earthquake, that the foundations of the prison were shaken. At once all the prison doors flew open, and everyone's chains came loose."
—Acts 16:26

Chapter 10

The Streets of Miami

My world of drugs in the fast lane

"Watch and pray so that you will not fall into temptation. The spirit is willing but the flesh is weak."
—Matthew 26:41

I had seven cars, two ice cream trucks, a mobile catering and more cash than anyone I have ever known.

I had more cash than anyone I had ever known, including two ice cream trucks, a mobile catering and seven cars. I have never been down or a man without a hustle. As a kid, I learned that, huh? I have never been homeless, even when I ran away at 13 years old after my father was shot and killed. My dad was tough as hell. My granddad and biological dad too. And I was gonna be just like them. No one was ever gonna touch me again. And the people on the streets knew it. They were all afraid of me. And I was successful. I had it all, just like my dad taught me when I was little. I was used to having nice things. And I had all of the money, women, things and freedom to do whatever I wanted. I loved being able to make my own choices. It was my way or no way. I had no choices in my life growing up. I had been powerless, but not anymore. Maybe I had seen so much of my father, uncle and Granddad as with their own money and businesses, that this is what I wanted in my life. Whatever the reason, I had my mind made up, huh? Only God can change my mind even today when I decide on something.

The strange thing is though, was that this, time in my life where I chose drugs and to walk my own way was right after God had delivered me from prison the second time. You would have thought that I would have changed my ways immediately with new wife and family. In fact, when I was released the second time, my first wife was delivering my son, huh? The guard told me to go to the hospital and take care of my newborn son and wife. I was grown when I got out of prison the second time I got out but I was still angry, even after God got released me. I tried to be a good man to my wife and father to my children but I was angry at many things, hmm? I was angry that as an ex-felon I could only make $8.00/hour. How was I to support a wife and kids on that? I mean, really? You are just left, locked up, to think about how to make your life great when you get out and get revenge. I knew that I would get revenge by making a lot of money and never being without again.

The penal system really messes up your life, or at least that is how I thought of it. I know that I was there because of my choices, but when you grow up like I did, you feel powerless and your choices don't seem like a lot. Try to imagine the world I grew up in, huh? A world where you had nothin' given to you, huh? You had nobody give anything to you, hmm? You had to work for everything, hmm? And even then, man, it was never enough, huh? Huh? I was young and had no father to show me how to navigate life or even to be a husband. I had no role models. My uncle gave me a good example but the hurt was still too much. And the ones I did have showed me how to make the money, how to hustle, but never how to do it a different way. I was trying to figure it all out on my own. On my own! With no guidance!

Right out of prison I went to dealing drugs and making a living for my family. I went from using drugs to selling drugs on the street to being a huge drug dealer.

My name was BOP.

BOP was my name. Shoot, some still call me that to this day. In every city that I have been in, I have gone by a different name, huh? And this was the name I had when I was in Orlando at twenty in 1988 and then in Miami. My name was well known. I was respected and feared, hmm? Those were my years of living a life that was not good, no. I was never gonna be taken advantage of again by nobody. And BOP didn't play, huh? People would see me pull up and they'd run. Literally. They would take off, huh? They didn't want to be anywhere around me. I was tough and nothin could get past me. Nothing. If BOP couldn't handle it on the streets, no one could. There ain't nothin I couldn't handle. And I wasn't afraid, just like when I was little. Not ever. And guess what, I never cried then either. BOP was not a nice person, not at all. He controlled his world. I was known by this name for many, many years. I was dealing drugs as BOP back then and I did that for over ten years. I did that for over ten years. I never got busted. I sold any drug I could get my hands on and I made over $200 a day and that was a good living for a man with three children and a wife. I wanted to always quit and I used to minister to the people on the street about Jesus. I felt so bad for them. I saw myself in them. I had no idea how to be a husband or a father I had not dealt with the things of my past, so I had and a great deal of hurt and anger that was growing in me, My first wife really put up with a lot from me. She was and is a great woman both in life and to our three children. We both did things that eventually ended our marriage. I was having affairs with other women while married, living the fast life and with no intention to quit.

After my first marriage, I met a woman who could run with me. I continued to make money selling drugs and running mobile BBQ and ice cream truck businesses. I had seven cars, one ice cream truck and a mobile BBQ. My business increased. I was dealing drugs but God had my heart and I was ministering to the people on the streets. Isn't that unbelievable, huh? Today, I minister to the people on the streets, too but God is my source for my income, huh? He was training me, even back then, huh? Training me for my future with him, huh? Huh? Many told me that I should not be selling drugs because I was too nice. God was instilling something deep in my heart what I would be doing in the future, hmm? And I learned to love the people on the streets too. That's where I get my deep love for them. A true and genuine love. Because I was one of them, huh? Isn't God amazing!

Well I was too busy living life my way and running my own show and eventually the woman I was with got pregnant, and relationship ended abruptly, although

I am very close to my daughter to this day. After my relationship ended with my daughter's mother, I met and married my very best friend and second wife. I had fallen in love with her years before and now we reconnected and were married. I was still in the drug world with my new wife. I had started speaking to Mama again after my divorce from my first wife. It took me that long to begin to let go of the hurt from my childhood and my anger toward Mama. That was close to two years. I finally began to understand all that Mama went through for me. She never told me back then, she just carried her hard burden all by herself. She is such a strong woman and so loving.

Well, with all of the money and cars and my new wife and I were having fun, but very soon, my time would be running out with God and it was then that God issued me a serious call. I was confident that I heard God correctly because by now I knew when God was speaking to me. God told me that I had a choice to make. I was either to turn my life over to him or I would die. He said that I could live or die, the choice was mine. Plain and simple. I knew without a doubt this was real. I knew His voice so well and that this was serious, my wife and I turned back to God and we set out on the road, giving and away everything we had, all of the drug money and all of the possessions bought with drug money. We were on the road for years and then we began rebuilding our lives. We turned to God for real. I mean for real. It was a long hard road but we did it together. We travelled to many different states and lived in a few homeless shelters before we settled down while we were rebuilding our lives God's way. We were homeless by choice, because I decided to take God seriously and give up my life of drugs. Deciding to live God's way meant giving up all that we had and starting over. I started working 3 jobs since 2003 and for 13 years we raised our two boys. She and I went our separate ways in 2016. I never went back to a life of drugs.

I will never forget God's words to me that "I needed to decide and make a choice." It is important to listen to God and obey. It is so important. God told me I needed to make a choice. Sometimes God has to take us down before bringing us back up in front of kings, to our rightful positions. But God never forgets about His called servants and he won't leave us there. No. God has rescued me, saved me, stopped me and redirected me so many times in my life. Yet the greatest times are when he breaks me down, for His glory. For only when we are fully broken can God finally use us. To bring the GLORY unto him. To bring the GLORY unto Him. Thank you, LORD!

"The son said to him, '
Father, I have sinned against heaven and against you.
I am no longer worthy to be called your son.'
But the father said to His servants, 'Quick!
Bring the best robe and put it on him.
Put a ring on his finger and sandals on his feet.
Bring the fattened calf and kill it.
Let's have a feast and celebrate.
For this son of mine was dead and is alive again;
he was lost and is found."
—Luke 15:11-32

Chapter 11

My 3:00 AM Meeting with God

God calls Marriese

*"For the revelation awaits an appointed time,
it speaks of the end and it will not prove false.
Though it linger, wait for it;
it will certainly come and will not delay.*

—Habakkuk2:3

It was 3:00 AM and God woke me up.

God woke me up at 3:00 AM. It was 1998 and I was living in Atlanta. This is what happened. I heard a man's voice calling me, but it said "Jeremiah." This was the first time, but since it was not my name, I went back to sleep. The man's voice called me a second time. It said "Jeremiah." I said, "That's not my name," and I went back to bed a second time. Then it happened again. This time I knew it was God. The voice said, "Jeremiah." I got up this time. God told me to go downstairs to my basement. When I went to the basement I grabbed my Bible and opened it. It opened to JEREMIAH 33. I read the scripture. This is the night that God called me as a Prophet of the LORD. God told me, "Tell them. Tell them and don't be afraid of their faces." No matter if they are kings, or family or church leaders or whoever, tell the people. Tell the people about Me! I cried all night, until 6am. I couldn't even go to work the next day. GLORY TO GOD. This is the night God called me as a Prophet of the LORD.

Jeremiah was a prophet in 626 B.C. and is in both books of the Bible of Lamentations and Jeremiah. He was a major prophet who was called by God before birth to go before all the nations of the ancient world. He was to call the people of that time to repent and turn back to God. That is my desire today. God has had His hand on my life before I was born. Here I was born and unwanted by my biological father. But God already knew and ordained why he would choose a father that was not wanting to claim me. See, the father in ancient times gives the name to the child or establishes the child's meaning by the name. Well watch this, God became my father, because my biological father was never supposed to establish me, because that was what God was going to do for me. God would set me aside for himself, so he had to be the one to establish me.

God is able to restore our purpose. God in one instant can establish us to who we were always meant to be. It doesn't matter how far off we have travelled from His path, when we submit to God, he will restore and redeem us. God was establishing me for His purposes since before my birth and He purposefully chose a biological father that would give me up so I could be a testimony for His glory. And although my biological father did not want to establish me with a name and a meaning, God did that through my mother! My name, Marriese Alexander, literally means dark-skinned warrior. My mother did not know that, but that is what I am and who God ordained me to be! I am a warrior and a soldier in God's army. This night, God told me who I was. God called me by a name that told me who I was and what I was to do for Him.

That night, my past was redeemed because to God, it did not alter my future. To God, my purpose in Him was still secure. And all He had to do was speak and by His Word, my life made sense. Because that is how God is. Nothing is too hard for God. No life is too far gone for God. And when we hear God speak our name and call us by who we are in Him, our purpose and our lives make sense. This is the reason I was born. To bring glory to God and to call the people back to him. And God developed my fearlessness and boldness that I would need for this calling through all I went through at an early age. I am afraid of no man and all I fear is God. So, I can preach it. Because I fear not what man can do or say to me. The minute God calls us, everything else is gone. When God calls us by our purpose and why we were created, everything in our past, present and future is redeemed. GLORY TO GOD. Therefore, every detail of my life was anointed for God's purpose. God is so cool! He is so awesome! Not long after I was called as a Prophet of the LORD, God gave me my non-profit, Hedges and Highway Outreach Ministries. God told me to go to the highways and byways and compel the people to come.

*"Abrahm believed the LORD
and it was credited to him as righteousness"*

—Genesis 15:6

Redeemed
By Big Daddy Weave

Seems like all I could see was the struggle
Haunted by ghosts that lived in my past
Bound up in shackles of all my failures
Wondering how long is this gonna last
Then you look at this prisoner and say to me,
"Son, stop fighting a fight that's already been won."

I am redeemed,
You set me free
So I'll shake off
These heavy chains
Wipe away every stain
Now I'm not who I used to be
I am redeemed,
I'm redeemed.

All my life I have been called unworthy
Named by the voice
Of my shame and regret
But when I hear You whisper,
"Child lift up your head"
I remember, oh God,
You're not done
With me yet.

I am redeemed

You set me free
So I'll shake off these heavy chains
Wipe away every stain
Now I'm not who
I used to be
Because I don't have to be
The old man inside of me
'cause his day is long dead and gone
Because I've got a new name,
A new life, I'm not the same
And a hope that will carry me
Home

I am redeemed. You set me free
So I'll shake off these heavy chains
Wipe away every stain
'cause I'm not who I used to be.

I am redeemed. You set me free
So I'll shake off these heavy chains
Wipe away every stain, yeah.
I'm not who I used to be.
Oh, God, I'm not who I used to be
Jesus I'm not who I used to be
'"cause I am redeemed
Thank God redeemed.

Part II
1980-1992

Reflections

12 Years

Chapter 12

A Mighty River Begins to Flow

God's river in my life

"That person is like a tree planted by streams of water, which yields its fruit in season and whose leaf does not wither, whatever they do prospers."

—Psalm 1:3

God saved all of my tears that I cried as a little boy and made a river for my life.

God made a river for my life. God saved all of my tears that I cried as a little boy. Could it be that God saves all of our tears and one day they will flow like a raging river for His purposes and His glory? I believe it, for I have seen it in my life. And God says it. "Record my misery; list my tears on your scroll-are they not in your record?" Psalm 56:8. How does a story like mine turn into a testimony for God? My story went from helplessness to rebelliousness to times of self-righteousness to chosen submissiveness. I chose to submit to God's will for my life and everything started to change. During this season of rebellion and turning back to God, He called me as a prophet, during this season. It was one of the most rebellious seasons of my life and God was right there. Waiting and wooing me back to him as he did that night using Jeremiah 33. God was telling me to: "turn back from desolation and I will make you abundant and with peace overflowing." God never left me. God never leaves. God is closest to us when we are afflicted and he rejoices with us when we return like the prodigal son. Boy, isn't God amazing? He is constantly wooing us back to him. Showing us that he is the water in our deserts. He was water in my ten years of deserts. And I never left him. I never left. And God knew that I never left. He knew I was just too hurt to go on at times and I detoured, that I was searching for answers and to make my life have some sense, some control. Was I searching for a father? And God says: "I am your father. I am your father. Come to me and I will give you rest."

I had some detours. I mean to tell you that my detours were huge. And God delivered me from them all. He is faithful in the wilderness. Oh, come on somebody. He had to take me through some very dark nights. Because I detoured and was trying to escape the pain within my own power. Those detours included drugs. My detours included being a thug. And doing things my own way. Sometimes our detours take years. But God is making us whole during those times. God is increasing our character during those dark nights. They are the dark nights of the soul! And although we may detour. He is keeping us through it all. During those detours if we look back, hmm, we can see God. God kept me during those years. He kept me. I have His protective hand. His hand covers my life! The call of God on my life cannot be stopped, just like the call of God on your life cannot be stopped.

This journey is so great and God is so amazing in my life with what he has delivered me from and is bringing me into. My life is so awesome! When I look back on it now, it is so amazing. God is a God of order. He had to bring me back to him first and get my mind and heart in the right place with him before I would get to the Promised Land. He said, "I must choose." Him or a life of drugs. That is what God said to me. Because until my life was in order, I could not receive the Promised Land. Because I wouldn't have known what to do with the Promised Land, until God got me ready, I was not ready for my Promised Land. It is too big! So, I had to go through it! And God is our real treasure anyway. He is our real "Promised Land." God tells us to not be like the world but have a renewing of our mind. The mind is flesh and so these were my struggles. But God says: "Oh that you stray for a little while, return to me oh faithless one and I shall restore you!"

These were the years that God called me and increased my passion and my desire for him first. These were my years where he commissioned me as a Prophet of GOD. And Jeremiah was the last prophet called and sent by God before the nation of Israel crumbled. They were in such rebellion against God. Jeremiah gavesthe final warnings. Jeremiah had a big job! Jeremiah preached for forty years. Jeremiah got discouraged in his work for God. God called Jeremiah back to him saying I will restore God. I am your living water. God also did that for me. God called me to Himself. Wow, man that is powerful! And the Prophet of God usually rebels. Because the call is so big! And because our sin nature, our flesh fights the spirit person. I have done my share of rebelling from my calling. What God had shown me was so big sometimes that I didn't want to do it! But the one thing that I know in my life, is that I am called of God. God has favor on my life. And he can break EVERY CHAIN in our life. Every chain! GLORY TO GOD

" It was You who opened up springs and streams;
you dried up the ever flowing rivers."
—Psalm 74:15

Break Every Chain
Tasha Cobbs

There is power
In the name of Jesus
There is power
In the name of Jesus
There is power
In the name of Jesus
To break every chain
Break every chain
Break every chain
To break every chain
Break every chain
Break every chain
There is power
In the name of Jesus
(You declare it)
There is power
In the name of Jesus
There is power
In the name of Jesus
(we know where it is)
To break every chain
Break every chain
Break every chain
To break every chain
Break every chain
Break every chain
There's an Army
Rising Up

There's an Army
Rising Up
There's an Army
Rising Up
To Break every chain
Break every chain
Break every chain
To break every chain
Break every chain
Break every chain
There's an Army
Rising Up
There's an Army
Rising Up
There's an Army
Rising Up
To break every chain
Break every chain
Break every chain
(The chains are broken, the chains are broken)
I hear the chains falling
I hear the chains falling
I hear the chains falling
(You gotta hear it)
I hear the chains falling
(hear it in the spirit, it's loud in my ear)
I hear the chains falling.

Chapter 13

All Things New

"I will make you a new heart and put a new spirit in you;
I will remove from you your heart of stone
and give you a heart of flesh"

—Ezekiel 36:26

God restored my heart.

My heart God restored. God is making everything
new. A heart of flesh and not of stone. That's what he
does. He makes a way in the desert when there is no
way. He makes all things new and restores all things, but
not only that, He makes what has never been before, be.
He is a creating God and He is constantly creating, see.
He's too big to just be making what was the same again,
no. He is making things come into being that never
were. Yeah, man. And that is what God told me. He is
turning things completely around. There is a new flow.
God told me everything is different. Man, that is God and
that is exciting!

The love that I have in my heart for people is great. Because I know what it feels like not to be loved. I know what it feels like to be hidden and not to be looked at as worthy enough to be claimed. I grew up with that in my household and I was hurting. I loved from the core of my heart, boy, and I would do anything for anybody. That is why I hurt so badly, when I didn't get the love. So now, I don't do that. I don't do that to people. If you are good to me and even if you are not good to me and everyone else doesn't like you or is against you, I'll claim you, because I am not embarrassed to stand up and tell everyone you're my friend and you're important to me. God did that for me. He never abandoned or rejected me. Even when everyone else rejected me, God claimed me now, yeah man. It is a terrible thing. Rejection. People today are dying from rejection and from those who are supposed to care about them, being rejected over and over again. I know, see? 'cause I grew up that way.

My biological father did that to me for so long, till I was almost grown. And I never knew I was important to him. I cried every day for the love that I didn't have from my family, from the very people that were supposed to give love. I did everything right as a kid, but I was unloved for who I was and that hurt me to my core. People today are hurting at their core because they don't feel the love. I will never reject you or be embarrassed to tell the world about you, no. I'm 100 percent about that. I'm the real deal. Jesus even ate with tax collectors and prostitutes. And he was betrayed by one of his closest friends, Peter, in his worst hour. Jesus forgave Peter but it took a long time for Peter to forgive himself. Because Peter had just gotten through telling Jesus how much he loved him and then he betrayed him, he denied him in front of the crowds. Peter would spend the rest of his life making up for it, preaching and identifying with his friend until he died. And then he died just like Jesus did, crucified but upside down. Because he was not worthy to be like Jesus. Don't do that to people. Don't do it, because Jesus didn't do it to you. God showed me through my past what not to do to others. That is why I have great love today. God's going to make me love them even if I don't want to.

My whole life people have to come to me with their problems. And I always said why are they coming to me? I am hurting and my family who was all love have stopped loving each other. And the envy was overtaking us. And we came from the same blood! And all you haters on me were all there for others. Man, that hurt me to my core, I'm telling you. And out of everybody's children? I was only one who experienced the abuse, the neglect and abandonment. So what did God do? God made me get to know Him. God makes people thirsty for Him. And that's what I was. I was thirsty for love of God, the love I didn't get from my family. And just like Joseph, when his brothers did him wrong.

God gave me an undying love for all my family. And I will do them no wrong. Because God said just do nobody no wrong and have love in your heart. Because that is how I love you. And that is how I forgave and forgive you. So, because I forgive like that, you are to forgive others like that. That is the agape unconditional love of God. For they know no better, of what they do now. They know not what they do. And so God said love them despite themselves, huh? And I do. And my love for them runs deep. And I don't care if they love me or not, because I'm gonna love the hell out of them, boy. Yeah, I am. I am going to love them just like Joseph loved his family. That is my calling. To love with an unconditional love of Jesus. Yes. Now, God gives me the understanding that I was being shaped for my life story and perfected in the image of the living God, saved by God and trained for His army. I know God's hand is on my life. I know for a fact that God is with me and saved me. Can't nobody tell me different either. God said, "Let not my righteous be touched, for your enemies will fall at your feet." I know that God has called me as His anointed and His prophet so there is double blessing on my life. God showed me back then that He was real. He brought me through all that.

"Remember not the former things nor consider the things of old. Behold I am doing a new thing; now it springs forth, do you not perceive it? I will make a way in the wilderness and rivers in the desert"

—Isaiah 43:18-19

Chapter 14

Called Into the Army of the Lord

Looking to the hills for God

"Woe to me!" I cried. '
I am ruined, for I am a man of unclean lips...
then one of the Seraphim flew to me with a live coal...
with it he touched my mouth...
Then I heard the voice of the LORD saying,
'Whom shall I send? And who will go for us? '
And I said, 'Here am I. Send me!'

—Isaiah 6:8

Man, God can change everything in an instant.

In an instant God can change anything. My favorite quote by my grandmother is "A bad wind can change." If we change our focus to God, God moves, boy! Uh huh! After my calling to be a prophet of God, my focus shifted. God was doing a new thing. Grandmother always said that quote to me and it means that anyone can change. And God is the one to change us. I always was a sensitive boy and had loved people to my core, although I didn't get the love. But God had His hand on my life before I was born. Before I was born I was set to be in the army of the LORD. And nothing nobody did to me was gonna change God's call on my life, or my great love for Him. I know I am strong and I am a survivor. God made me that way. I had to be! I had no choice! And when God told me that my hand is anointed and everything I touch is anointed, I knew I had to work for God. When God gave me my non-profit, that was it. I knew how blessed I was to be working for God. I was a thug and God called me for who I was ordained to be before birth. Now, I just had to walk it out.

A bad wind can change. Yeah, man. My passion and my calling is my non-profit and working for God. Hedges & Highway Outreach Ministries must come first in my life and God has big plans for this ministry. I love feeding people my food but even more than that, I love giving spiritual food. I believe that God has given me many gifts that He expects me to use for HIS glory. I believe that like Joseph's coat of many colors, Hedges & Highway Outreach Ministries will be serving people across the country in many different ways, that is why I call it ministries. I believe that I am being sent by God and to follow Him.

We arrived in Denver in 2001. I asked my wife for the map because we didn't know where to go. My wife wouldn't give me the map, because she knew God would tell us. My wife and I placed our hands on a map and we prayed over it. My thumb was on Colorado and hers was on Pennsylvania. We decided to come to Colorado. We followed God's direction, trusting the LORD. When we arrived, I had expected a childhood friend to meet us and give us and our two young boys shelter. He never showed up. A local clerk at a gas station pointed us to a local Salvation Army. We stayed there two months and I worked three jobs to support us until we got an apartment of our own.

For the next 13 years, I worked three jobs to support my family and waited on God's promise. I kept it moving forward. Although the vision tarried, God says wait for it for it will surely come. I worked three jobs for 13 years. Thirteen years! Man, this promise by God for Hedges and Highway and Anointed took me over 13 years to see come into fruition to its fullness. But during that time, God was training me on the streets of Denver. He paid me to do it too. Watch this! So, God has me build a street ministry with Aurora Mental Health with their street homeless program. So, I am walking the streets and building relationships with those that God will have me minister to with Hedges and Highway in the future, but He is paying me to do it. Isn't God awesome how He brings everything together? And before Aurora Mental Health, He has me running all of the volunteers and kitchen at the Denver Rescue Mission. Over 30 volunteers and He also has me work for the Hyatt and the Crowne Plaza. I ran entire shifts by myself for huge hotels, because that's my element. But now He is having me lead people in the Denver area so they can see and know my leadership. And all that I built with the Denver Rescue Mission, all the connections and all of the programs that I built for them would be used in the future for my own restaurant. Then, God had me work for the Salvation Army. I cooked here for 33 homeless families and developed their kitchen and their programs. I did this while I was a Case Manager with Aurora Mental Health. So, I was doing the work that I would do with my own business and non-profit in the future, but God was having me work out all of the kinks, gaining experience and doing with someone else's business, while I was getting paid and supporting my family. See, wherever God has you in life, don't give up. There is a reason and a purpose for you being there, God is working out all of the details behind the scenes for you. He is faithful. Wow. God is FAITHFUL!

During this time, God gave me the people to get Hedges and Highway's official 501 (c) 3, non-profit status! We started with our first Board of Directors and began having our meetings and do outreach with Hedges and Highway Outreach Ministries. God had begun to develop my vision and my wife and I began to move forward with this vision. It was an exciting time and although not everything had come into being yet, we were ministering to the people. I was asked to be a guest at church events and I helped partner with other churches and outreaches to build the kingdom of God. My spirit man was being used and developed at this time as a prophet of God and I made incredible friendships and partnerships with the Denver people. So many people in Denver wanted to support me and the ministry! Some top leaders of the Colorado Rockies told me that they would support my vision and my work. Other leaders in the community became good friends. Denver was becoming a place of abundance for my family and me. This was a true time of blessing of the LORD. More would come as my network increased in the Denver area. God was also increasing my connections with other non-profit organizations! These partners would become my partners with Hedges and Highway. It was all coming together.

I have connections now everywhere, too. God had me in Atlanta, in Alabama, in Georgia...in places all over the country because He knew that Hedges and Highway (H & H) and Anointed BBQ & Soul food would be worldwide someday. And God was also establishing me with the Body of Christ in places all over the country too. You see God is multi-dimensional, He's not just working one area, He's working them all together so ALL things will work to the good of those who love God. All things! God had first me connect with my Bishop in Alabama, who is my spiritual father and mother, before bringing me to Denver. God was strategizing! He is a strategist and the best kind! He knew that Denver would be my home, but that I was called to travel. And I would need other hubs of refreshment and spiritual nourishment. So, all of these things would be established and put into place ahead of my dream coming into reality. This is so when it all comes together in perfection and order, we can give the glory only to GOD. Because God wants all the Glory. God gets all the GLORY in my life too, boy!

"Then Jesus told his disciples, '
If anyone would come after me,
let him deny himself and take up his cross
and follow me."

—Matthew 16:24

Part III
(1992-2017)

Memories of Mo Jones

Chapter 15

A Restaurant and a Movement

*"Go then, eat your bread in happiness
and drink your wine with a cheerful heart;
for God has already approved your works."*
—Ecclesiastes 9:7

When God says move forward, one must move ...

One must move when God says move forward. I am meant to be an entrepreneur. I am like my biological father and my granddad in that way. I can run things and build a vision, huh? **Anointed BBQ & Soul Food** was just one promise that God gave to me. God had already given me the name of **Anointed BBQ & Soul Food** in 2000. He told me that there was love and healing in the food, huh? That the people would be healed, hmm? God said the food will show my passion and that the people will taste the love.

I saw the location that God told me would be my restaurant well before it happened. Now there was already a barbecue restaurant operating there, so this would require spiritual eyes and faith for me to still believe in God's promise to me. Kind of like when the Israelites were told that the Promised Land of Canaan would be theirs, but it was already inhabited when they got there after their long journey! So, the restaurant that God was fixin' to give me, well it was being run by another black man as a BBQ restaurant! Yet, I was so confident in God's promise and Word to me about this restaurant location, at 2504 W. Hamden Avenue in Sheridan, Colorado that I knew it would be mine. I knew! Yeah, man. I just did not know when, hmm? So, I knew the location of my first restaurant before it ever became mine. Wow! I knew God wouldn't lie to me now, huh, He was fixin to give me that building, huh? So, I went to the restaurant and offered to come on and help the man. See, I was trying to make it happen in my time and my way 'cause I believed God so much, huh? I offered to partner with that man, hmm? I was a chef and I told him I could take him to the next level. But, the owner of the restaurant was prideful and I saw it in him, hmm? But although I saw his pride, I asked him anyway. He wouldn't take me up on my offer, huh? So, I thought okay! That's okay, huh? Because God's fixin' to give me this entire building. Now, I don't know when, huh, but it's gonna happen, hmm? Because God told me and there ain't nothin you can do, huh? Huh! So, I left MY restaurant and knew that in the proper time, it would be mine. Yeah. "If it seems slow do not despair, for these things will surely come to pass. Just be patient! They will not be overdue a single day!" Habakkuk 2:3

I knew God's promise to me, because God had trained me in His faithfulness, huh? He could trust me with this vision, see. He could trust me to wait on Him.

And I would wait, see? 'Cause I knew God was working ALL things out for my good, huh? So, if God says not now, then I'm good, huh? Because God says all things are working for the good of those who love God, huh? You see, if I had not learned to trust Him earlier in life, how could He give me a vision that would require absolute faith! Glory!

So, after praying over that building I left that day and in 2014 the building was abandoned and the restaurant owner had left. Faithfully, every month in 2014-2015 for a year, I called the landlord of that building where **Anointed BBQ & Soul Food** birthed its first flagship store at 2504 W. Hamden Ave, Sheridan, CO and told the landlord that if she ever would consider renting it to me, I would be ready to accept it. Do you know that the landlords told me every month for a year that they were going to sell the building? Then in August of 2015, they began talking to me. In November 2015 the keys were picked up and **Anointed BBQ & Soul Food** took possession of 2504 W. Hamden Ave! God is faithful!

Trusting God when the struggle continued while waiting on the promise

While waiting on the promise, I trusted God when the struggle continued. For 15 years I waited on God's promise and worked multiple jobs, all the while fully knowing that the promise would come at the appointed hour and not a minute before. When it finally happened, I had to be equally discerning. You see, just because God was giving me **Anointed BBQ's** brick and mortar building did not mean that it was going to be easy, huh? Shoot, this has been some of the hardest days of my life opening this restaurant. We must not get confused when God brings us to our Promised Land. We must not think that the road is easy or without struggle, see. If we do, we may miss it, huh? We may think it is too hard, huh? But God gets us ready to take the land, huh? He says some of you're Promised Lands are gonna require some sweat and tears, yeah. Some of y'all will need to take your Promised Land by force, huh? By force! God got the Israelites ready in the desert, see. And they learned to rely on God for their Promised Land. Canaan would require some faith, huh? Those people of God had to drive out all of the people who were inhabiting it illegally, oh, come on, somebody! See, some of your Promised Lands that God promised you are being inhabited illegally by squatters! They think they can have what God promised you, huh? But, it's not their promise! And when God is ready, He will lead you to drive out those trying to take your blessing, 'cause God's blessing is for you, hmm? And ain't no one can steal your inheritance from the LORD. Man, that's powerful. GLORY TO GOD. You see so often we think that the Promised Land of "milk and honey" means easy or the most abundant. In Israel, Canaan was the land that God called the Israelites to go and inhabit. Although this land was and is the cradle of the ancient world with plush valleys and water resources, hmm, however it was not the absolute most fruitful land. But it was the land God was to give them. What would have happened it the Israelites had disobeyed God and chosen a land that they felt was better? They would have missed their calling!

You see, what God has for you is for you, huh? Your Promised Land may not be perfect, but it is what God is giving you! To fulfill his call on your life, you must move when God tells you to move, huh? So, it is with **Anointed's** first building. With no money, no resources, no equipment to run a restaurant, a lost job and lost apartment and a run-down building that needed major repairs, I took the building knowing that somehow God would come through. Somehow, the first month's rent would be paid in just a few weeks. I may not have the money now, huh, but God will make it happen, hmm? God is faithful, boy! God is faithful!

I trusted God about **Anointed BBQ & Soul Food**. He told me. He was gonna give me this building. So, when it came, I took it. I moved on that, boy! Yeah, man! I needed trust that although God's timing was not my timing, and move when He said move, huh? Would I go where God wanted me to go even though I may want to go a different way? Yes, I would! I was excited about the building and knew I wanted it! I could see the future because God has showed me. Yeah, man!

Daily Continued Struggles

Struggles continued daily. The way seemed unclear most times. Not some of the time, all the time! But, I knew the dream that God had placed deep in my heart was real and my dream was in my hand, yet so many times I was unclear of how it would come to pass. But if God started it man, I could be sure He was gonna finish it! I took a day job and was working day and night, boy! Day and night! I would then go and work long nights at the restaurant renovating it and begin to set up for **Anointed** to take shape, huh?

I cannot tell you enough how great the struggle was! I knew I had heard God and I knew his promise was coming true for me, however the daily grind was so heavy that at times, I wondered what God was doing! Now I see that God had to strip me even more than I had been stripped through my childhood struggles growing up in Miami. God had to strip me more than when I was in prison, huh? God had my biggest promise ahead and He needed to be certain that I was ready, huh? This promise was the beginning to all the other blessings and work that God will give to me. I had to learn to rely just on Him and not myself.

I did think that the renovation would be quick. I picked up the keys to the restaurant in November of 2015 and I thought it would be opened by January 2016. But, God had more for me to do before he would give me my dream. He needed to be with me in the struggle of the next six months. It would be August 4, 2016 before **Anointed BBQ & Soul Food** would actually open its doors. Everyday had so many challenges that it felt like ten years of struggle. There were moments when it took intense concentration to stay the course and believe. Because whenever you are moving toward your promise and your dream, there will be dream killers and haters, huh? I'm keepin it real man. But you got to trust God and move forward, huh? With nothin but God's word in your mouth. You must speak it! Speak God's promise to you! God placed people around me like my mama, my children, Rusty and Mr. Bud to breathe his life into my dream daily to encourage me. Yet the minute-by-minute battle was tough! But just as fast as the struggle, God provided.

God's Amazing Provisions

The provisions of God's were amazing. I took the building and accepted the lease. Not soon after, the challenges began to come, hmm? First, I lost my job with an apartment community that gave me a free apartment as one of my benefits. But then, just as fast as the obstacle came, an answer came. A man gave me a place to live and opened up his entire home to me with no money, huh? He just said, "Mo, open your dream." Man, that Rusty gave me his home and a place to live in the shed he made into a mother in law house. This shed became my home for over a year! God was providing and giving me blessings all around me. Rusty encouraged me in my dream and stood by me through my divorce. What a friend I have in Rusty, huh? He is like my brother! He has been a part of *Anointed BBQ* from the beginning, huh? Rusty helped with marketing, printing and setting up numerous catering events for *Anointed* before the doors even opened! Rusty helps in our outreaches and he gave us the $1000 needed to buy food and to open the doors on the first day of business in August 2016! The road was hard and long, yes! Another great provision of God was my non-profit. Yeah man. Years ago, God birthed my non-profit "*Hedges and Highway Outreach Ministries.*" This has always been my passion and my first priority. God brought important people together to be a part of launching the non-profit years before, when I was still married. But in the fall of 2015, right before *Anointed BBQ* got our building, I expanded the vision of *H & H*. This vision was so big that I secured an office in Aurora, Colorado for *Hedges & Highway Outreach Ministries*. Would you believe that part of the plan that God gave me for *H & H* was to begin to develop communities by starting restaurants? Huh? Then, before I knew it, the landlords of 2504 W. Hamden Ave gave us the building. When God says, "Move", we must be ready to move, hmm? We had the restaurant as an Extreme Community Makeover for *Anointed BBQ's* new location. Heading out with just fliers in my hand, I went to every Home Depot and Loews in the state of

Colorado and enlisted them to be a part of this great vision and great community restaurant that would serve the community.

How God Continued to Build Anointed BBQ

*Anointed BBQ God continued to build. A**nointed BBQ & Soul Food*** as a for profit business to empower the community in a very different way! By impacting the community from travelers coming to **Anointed** from all over the state of Colorado, money would be donated at local gas stations, coffee stores, retail outlets. Visions were set in motion that the restaurant would feed the homeless, offer help to give jobs and work with other local agencies to strengthen their missions. God allowed **H & H** to build **Anointed BBQ & Soul Food** in very tangible ways. By donating paint, paint brushes, pans, rollers, masking tape, nails, tables, chairs, benches, plants, signs, ropes, tiles, bathroom fixtures, umbrellas and much more, the **Anointed** truly is a community restaurant today and God and the community built it! God is so amazing.

God promoted Anointed BBQ daily during our building period

During our building period God promoted Anointed BBQ daily. God allowed the story of **Anointed** to be told to every person who gave any donation, huh? And not only that, but He made it so not one place gave more than a few items. While this could seem hard at times, because I had to so many places to go to, everyday God would not allow that, huh? Because He wanted the story to be told over and over again to many people, huh? Of how God was faithful, hmm? Faithful in the wilderness, huh? God wanted the story to be told! And every time

I said it, hmm, I believed it more and more, huh? HUH? God wanted people to know! God was using *Anointed* to bring the people together! If I would have waited until I had the financing or waited until I had a perfect restaurant, huh, then the story would not have been told. Your Promised Land is the one God wants YOU to have, hmm? It may not look like much to the average person, but God wants to make himself known to the people through you and what he is doing in your life! And it is all for HIS GLORY! Don't miss your PROMISED LAND because it may not look like what you think it should look like! Take the chance! Move forward! Listen to God!

The final push

The final push. So, although God was providing daily, I still had days where I was discouraged. I am human and there were days that it looked like it just was not going to happen. I was tired, huh? Even after all I did and overcame in my life, even after working three jobs for 13 years, this was by far the hardest task that I had ever accomplished. Since November 2015, every day was like a month's worth of work and stress! I wanted to quit stretching for my Promised Land so many times. Yeah, man! It was just too hard! There were days I wanted it to look different. I wanted to go and create it a better way. With a perfect building, huh? There were days when I had no car. I would leave the shed that I was living in and have to walk to the restaurant. I was fighting an enemy every day in my mind! The enemy would try to discourage me by telling me I had no money, no place to live, no job, no car, little food and a beat- up building. He tried to tell me my dream would not happen. I cried out in that basement of the restaurant for so many nights!

But God kept making me rely on His ways and not mine. God wanted me to sit and rest in Him and wait on Him. When I would wait on him, God would move. And God moved fast!

Another challenge was getting the sign on our property painted. We needed a lift and to at least cover up the lettering from the last owner. To rent a lift was expensive and we had no money for that. One afternoon, I walked out the back door of the restaurant and there was a woman there with her truck. That lady said to me, "I was just wondering if you needed someone to get up there and paint your sign? " Huh? She only wanted some BBQ and a little bit of money. That lady said that to me, boy! These things would happen all the time! These "God moments" gave me encouragement and let me know that God was opening this building!

We had an event November 2016 before the restaurant was opened. This event was our first November Neighborhood Outreach to the community to let people know that we were in the neighborhood and introduce them to **Anointed BBQ** and the nonprofit **Hedges and Highway Outreach Ministries**. The restaurant would not be operating to cook food, so we were catering it in from a commissary kitchen where I prepared all the food. Three days before the event, we had a local car dealership donate a car to give-away. They just gave it to us, huh? Who does that? Who gives a car? Man, that's God! This would be our big promotion that would draw attention and bless a member of the community! The event went off without a hitch and we had 12 local recruiters present food bags and clothes for the homeless. The Denver Fire Department came and supported us and we were able to air this on FOX NEWS!

Look at God! This was one of the happiest moments of my life. I felt like I had honored my grandmother and my dream was coming to pass!

Another God provision was Mr. Bud. Mr. Bud came to **Anointed** in the end months before the restaurant opened. Mr. Bud is a blessing, boy! He is a retired restauranteur, handyman, carpenter and electrician who guided me through my building code inspections, with low costs that I could afford. My long-time friend Paul and his wife helped to pull up old tile and renovate the bathroom. My uncle Arthur came to help build out parts of the restaurant and cook with me at a fundraiser one month after we attained the building in 2016. A donation of equipment from Bob and Pam Scala placed sinks, pans, stoves, tables and chairs into the building. Wow! God was blessing us through the people!

Opening day and a year later

A year later, **Anointed** is still growing strong and our customer base is amazing. People have been so good to us, huh? We have loyal customers and volunteers who just love what we are doing and love **Anointed**! *(See the appendix section at the back of the book for some customer comments).* Every day we serve customers with love that nourishes the soul and food that feeds the body, huh? We partner with Urban Peak to feed homeless teens on the weekend. Two of my close friends Louella and Mary Ellen lead that outreach ministry and it is a blessing! We have a men's group called, "The Men of Struggle," Men from the community come together to share and support each other. We have had singing groups sing for us at the restaurant and have a loyal following. All of our advertising up to this point has been word of mouth. This year has been such a blessing. Different family and friends came to help with the opening of **Anointed BBQ & Soul Food**. I just "kept it moving" and on August 4, 2016, *Anointed BBQ & Soul Food's* doors were officially opened. When I served our first customer, that was a happy moment for me.

"For he has satisfied the thirsty soul, And the hungry soul he has filled with what was good."

—Psalm 107:9

Part III

A Wise Mo Looks Ahead...

(1992-2017)

Today's Reflective Essays

Chapter 16

Water & Fishing

Mo Fishing Today

*"Come, follow me", Jesus said,
and I will send you out to fish for people."*

Matthew 4:19

Fishing still is what I love to do....

What I still love to do is fish. And I continue to fish to this day, huh? Looking back, I remember how everyone would make fun of me and say that I was crazy to pull those strings out of my grandmother's rug and put them on the end of a switch to make a fishing pole. I mean it was kind of funny that they all would laugh at me. Yeah, man. My grandmother would tell them to leave me alone. I didn't care if they laughed at me. That's why I don't care what anyone thinks of me or what they say about me today. I used to fish in the muddy waters of the cattails by my grandma's house. It was the only place I could go that I wouldn't cry The only place! I cried every day when I was home alone in my bed. Fishing is a part of who I am and it helped make me who I am today. Fishing also reminds me of Grandma because it was there or in her house that I found happiness of any kind back then. Grandma taught me so much.

Today fishing is one of the places where I go to find true peace. Fishing has such a different meaning for me today, and yet still gives me the same comfort as it did back then. It is one of the places where I can go and hear God and get clarity. The other place is in my kitchen. Fishing is my safe place. I don't go as much as I would like today. But today God urges me to "Come follow Him and be a fisher of men." Isn't that great? God knew what he was doing way back then! God met me in the silence in the muddy waters of the cattails' fishing hole. And it was only a hole! God was there, giving me peace and strengthening me as a young boy to have the confidence in Him that he could and would deliver me and save me.

God can meet us in our deepest sadness and he sees all that we go through. When we are weak he is strong. My God lifted me out of the mire and the muck. He set my feet upon a rock and He put a new song in my mouth that would build me as his prophet. He took many years to develop my story, yet, He didn't waste any of it. As I was becoming a man through the seemingly endless days and nights of suffering, there was this place of still waters for my soul and that was my experience when I was fishing. Among all of the turbulent waves, fishing became my place of refuge and strengthening. God made his presence so tangible and real for me there. My place of refuge. My fishing hole.

Mama always said that water has a special meaning and a power when mixed with prayer. God says come to the water of life and you will never be thirsty again, huh? The water cleans us spiritually too, hmm? It's powerful. I believe that God was restoring me and everything in me when I went to that fishing hole, huh? Hmm? It was my place of restoration. It was where God made me strong to go back to my situation, huh? He was then and is now my living water, huh? He was the place I went and was sheltered and although I was suffering, huh. Oh, come on somebody. I was filled with living water at that early age, huh? Huh? Wow. That's powerful. My God. I wonder at times if he purposefully left me alone, so I would have to turn to Him? Of course. As a kid I didn't think that way but today, I wonder. What the devil meant for bad, God used for good and to train me to trust Him. "And he hid me in the cleft of his wing" When I go home, Mama wants to go fishing. So, I take her and we go together. Mama catches more fish than I do. We fry them up of course, for dinner or breakfast.

My grandmother was one that was fishing for people, huh? She taught me how to love unconditionally. She reached out to hurting people, hmm? My grandmother was a lady that was gonna love you, huh? No matter what you did, she was gonna love you. She was loyal to my granddad. That was the only man she ever was with. She had 17 kids and raised them and the grandkids! My grandmother didn't play, huh? Her love was fierce, hmm? And she believed in you. Yeah, she taught me how to love fierce. And she was gonna tell you her mind. But then she was gonna love you anyway, huh? My grandmother was everything in my world. I was her favorite. I knew that. Boy, did she love me. Wow. My grandmother gave me so much of what I am today. She used to always say to me, "It's going to be okay." Those were her words to me. And I believed her and guess what, huh? It finally is. Today, everything is okay. But back then, wow! Well, I didn't know. The love is what my grandmother is remembered for. Her love made a huge impact on my life and the way that I love people. I am starting the **Maggie Jones Hope & Healing Foundation** this year because Grandmother brought so much hope and healing to people through her love and food. My Grandmother's legacy will carry on.

My granddad, Solomon Jones, was well respected in the community. My granddad was tough and the patriarch of the Jones family. One lesson that Granddad had taught us was not to lie. He always told us that a liar then could be a thief and could kill us. We knew that if we lied, we were gonna get a whooping. But if we told the truth, huh, then he would forgive anything. I will always remember that. I live by that today. My granddad was always clean too, hmm? He had the Jones "swag" that we all have today, huh? We were never to go out of the house dirty. We were always looking clean, us Joneses. Yeah, when I think of my fishing roots, I think of my roots, Grandma and Granddad.

"Therefore, go and make disciples of all nations, baptizing them in the name of the Father and of the Son and of the Holy Spirit, and teaching them to obey everything I have commanded you."

—Matthew 28:19-20

Chapter 17

He Is My Mouthpiece

"He will speak to the people for you, and it will be as if he were your mouth and as if you were God to him."

—Exodus 4:16

I know God is real and ain't nobody gonna shut my mouth.

Ain't Nobody is gonna shut my mouth for I know God is real. My mouth is my gift. God told me that He is speaking through me. And I am not gonna let anyone detour me from my gifts and my calling, huh? Hmm? You see I got to speak the truth, hmm? And I'm going to speak it with boldness and as God gives it to me, huh? Because God has always told me to speak the truth in love. And through my mouth and my gift will come my blessing. For no man's going to stop the river flow of what I have to say for God. The Holy Ghost has given me a Word and I'm gonna preach it to the whole world, huh? You better hear what I am saying. Oh, come on somebody! Jesus! Praise God!

As a little boy, no one listened to me. My grandmother did. But that was about it, hmm? Shoot, those people didn't care about me, huh? But she listened. From an early age, the devil was trying to steal my gift, huh? He was trying to make sure I felt like no one cared or would listen to me, huh? But God opened my mouth and He gave me what to say. And all of that hurt that I had pushed down is coming up like a raging river. But not to condemn, but to heal, hmm? All that was pushed down is now coming up for His GLORY.

Can you imagine growing up thinking that your own mother didn't want you because she was never there? hmm? And then my biological father hid me, hmm? I mean he was there, but I didn't know that he was my father, huh? He hid me. He had another family and I wasn't good enough to be talked about or acknowledged. That left me with such shame as a teen that I wasn't good enough to be wanted. And my stepfather's beatings? Can you imagine growing up and starting out like that? I suffered so much as a kid and my crying every day of my life for my mother was so damaging to me as a kid, and so much of that tried to hinder me throughout my life. But God wouldn't let it. God healed and restored that and restored my mother and I. We have the best relationship, huh? She is my best friend. As a kid and I didn't understand a lot back then of what she was going through and how difficult it was on her. I only knew what I felt and it was so painful to me, to not feel any love. But God reconciled us in the most amazing way and now I am her greatest supporter to this day. See God has done so much in every area of my life. And I am gonna tell it, hmm? Every kid needs love. I felt no love and my entire family was all about love and I felt none of it. That was painful!

I grew up with that every day of my life! That pain was overwhelming. That stuff there, it almost shut my mouth for good! Wow, what the devil tried to do to me! But God! Wow. When I would be with my grandmother cooking or when I was fishing alone was the only time I did not cry. That was some stuff there I went through, boy. That was some stuff! From an early age!

And then the tragedy of what happened on my birthday? I didn't want no birthday for so many years! I didn't celebrate and no one cared, hmm? Those people didn't care about me, huh? They ignored what I had been through and how deeply it affected me and how deeply it shattered me. And I had to grow up that way and process it all myself, huh? There was no one there to help me through it. All the trauma, hmm? There was no counseling for me. And to survive it the way I did, huh? With no medication, hmm? To come out of it with a sound mind. Now that is God, huh? Hmm? That is God, yeah. God became my father, hmm? He raised me! He was all I had! And he loved me, boy! And he does today! I KNOW God loves ME, huh? I KNOW! Yeah. He LOVES ME! And I'm gonna tell the world of what God did for me, hmm? Nobody can stop me now! No man can shut my mouth, PRAISE GOD. No mere man can stop the river's flow of what God has called me to be, THANK YOU LORD. He has called me to be a prophet, a preacher and an evangelist for the Almighty God, PRAISE GOD. The devil wanted to shut my mouth from an early age, boy. But God used it all for his GLORY. Amen. The devil meant to do me some harm, boy. But GOD? Anything that happens to me, will be used for my good, THANK YOU LORD. For the one who loves the Lord, hmm. Oh, come on now somebody! Thank you, Lord. God has turned my life completely around.

I am a strong tower of God and I will stand for righteousness and fight for the people. This is the call that God has given me. To tell the people about Him. To build leaders for the LORD. To plant churches across the country. God told me He gave me the story and no one can tell it better than me. I have been made by God to spiritually and naturally lead. I have to train up the young people. He gave me a love for the people like Christ. He makes me see what they are doing and to still love them. He made me into a person to lead and to plan and after all I went through, I didn't plan anything. God broke everything down to me on a deep level. This is what I am called to do. To build his church. Some people think I am crazy because I will be going one way and then just change directions. What they don't know is that I follow God's voice more than anyone else's.

The church problems that I experienced.

I experienced church problems. I was searching for a father figure in my life because I had no father. So, I went to the church. And the church hurt me over and over. And I still helped them build their house and no one ever supported me, hmm? This is some hard talk, boy. Yeah, they were taking advantage of a good person who was crying out for help in the wilderness and they prostituted my gift for money for their church. I was looking for a father and the churches prostituted my anointing and wouldn't father me and were jealous of my anointing, huh. God won't allow a whole lot in His house and one is theft. He won't tolerate thieves and leaders who are thieves and stealing the anointing and then using it for themselves, huh? Huh? God said I will make them give it back to you a 100 fold, hmm? And That's what God is doing, huh? God said to me keep giving it to people as I give it to you, huh? And God will give it back to me, hmm? So that's what I did, hmm. I'm keepin it real now, huh? I am not sugar coating anything. See, even Peter said, 'We must give it to people as I give it to you, huh? And God will give it back to me, hmm? So that's what I did, hmm. I'm keepin it real now, huh? I am not sugar coating anything. See, even Peter said, 'We must obey God rather than men.'"

One year we had 13 family members die. Thirteen. And not one pastor could find the time to come visit my family, hmm? They did not even visit my grandmother, huh? Boy that hurt me, man. I was done with the church after that, huh? I was done. But God would not let me be done, huh? He let me see it now, huh? Those fake people, huh? That didn't have the love, huh? And they were the church, Hmm? The body of CHRIST, huh? And they were jealous! They were jealous! Man, I'm telling you. The body of CHRIST is broken, hmm. See there are many parts to the BODY. And we are all to do our own part, huh? And come together as the BODY, hmm? One is an arm, one is a leg, one is a hand, hmm? And we are to function together, hmm? But the church forgets that. Because some preachers want it all for themselves. They want to do it all and have it all. Wow! The church that God is building through me, huh? It's different. There is an Apostolic calling on my life now, huh? And it took me a long time to get there, hmm? God holds me and keeps me, but every now and then, huh, there is a crack and I fall through, hmm? But God brings me back to himself quickly, huh? God does it quick! PRAISE GOD! And after he brings me back and establishes me again, he gives me his visions and gives me an even greater call than before, hmm? He says well done my good and faithful servant. You have passed the test. Now I can trust you with more. Now I can trust you with my church.

My mind is made up. And a mind that is made up is the spring to life. Because a double-minded man is unstable in all his ways. A double-minded man cannot stand, hmm? Huh? Huh? You better hear what I am saying. God says, settle it, huh? 'cause once it is settled and our minds are made up, things start happening. Once we settle it, God can finally work through us because we are fixed and not unstable in our ways. Yeah, it all comes together. God wants us to settle it in our minds. We need to make a decision about which way we will go in life, on many things. Recently, God told me that I needed to decide. That I needed to make a decision. I love that, because God gives us the choice, hmm? Free will to go the way he wants or the way we want, huh? That meant something to me. God was saying the time is now. And once the devil knew my mind was made up? Boy, I'm telling you, he was mad! So, whatever you are struggling with, huh? Settle it! Decide. See, the devil wants to keep you in confusion and disorder, but God is a God of order, huh? So settle it and let God work His perfect plan. Nothing can change God's plans now, hmm? But do your part, huh? Do what God is telling you to do and let Him write the story. The devil could do me no harm, hmm. Because I am God's chosen mouthpiece, huh? I am God's banner, his prophet, his representative, his agent, his delegate, his spokesman. I am God's banner. And I'm gonna build his church, hmm. The time is now and the people are excited. And ain't nobody going to distract me now. Ain't nobody going to shut my mouth from telling what God is to me. No.

"A double minded man is unstable in all of his ways."

—James 1:8 KJB

Chapter 18

For Such a Time as This

Raised up for a purpose

"For if you remain silent at this time,
for relief and deliverance
for the Jews will arise from another place,
but you and your father's family will perish.
And who knows that you have come
to your royal position for such a time as this."

—Esther 4:14

God said to me, now I built the story and nobody tells the story better than you.

Nobody will tell the story better than you, God said to me. I built the story. Now, walk in kingship. I know I have been chosen. I know that God chose me. I know that He has plans for me. I know He favors me and chooses me for a purpose, to serve Him. For a calling. And the call is great. And with a great call comes a great trial, huh? For me it was my entire life. My trial has been my whole life. But the calling is so heavy and the work is so important that the suffering had to refine me and attune my ears to the things of the LORD. To get me ready for such a time as this. God built my story, hmm? And now I have to tell it to the whole world. The people must know about God.

Timing is everything.

Everything is about timing. God told me about my gifts and dreams and what I would be doing well in advance of when my dreams came to pass. But I never gave up on God, Huh? God has always spoken to me and told me of things to come and I learned to hear and trust Him from the time I was a boy. But my dream was for a time such as this. The people are ready now, the landscape is ready to receive me now and, most of all, I am ready now. God had to get me ready to walk in the Promised Land. I wouldn't have been ready for this time, years ago, huh? No. I had to go through the fire. God had more for me to go through. He was making me into the man and warrior that I am today. It took forty years of God's training to make me into the man I am today! Forty Years! For God to take Moses from the Prince of Egypt to the Servant of God, it took forty years in the wilderness as a shepherd. God had to break down everything Moses was, all his assumed rights of privilege growing up in the most powerful kingdom in the ancient world. In the wilderness, Moses learned to be humble and to rely totally on God. When he was broken enough, he was ready to be used by God for the most important task that a man takes on in the Bible outside of Jesus. I had to be remade. These last years I felt like humpty dumpty, broken. God had to put me back together again, but in His way. There was more I had to go through. More I had to trust God for so I would be ready for where He is taking me. We have to trust the process.

Denver is my home now.

My home now is Denver. I am from Miami, but God told me that Denver is my main headquarters now. I tried to leave three times over the last 15 years, because there are parts of Denver I don't like. The ground is hard spiritually. It's very hard. Compared to the south, it's dry. And the culture. There is no comparison to the culture down south. But God keeps bringing me back. Maybe I'm back to change things here in Denver. Maybe it's gonna take a black man who is a business owner and a prophet to change the landscape here, huh? I'm going to run for City Council. I am believing God that I will be a mayor of a city. Why? Because God told me so. God said to me that He holds all the pieces, huh? He is putting everything into my hands.

God did some important things for me in Denver. Denver is where I got free. Denver is where I found my freedom at. I couldn't get free until I came to Denver, huh? 'cause this is the place that He is building my blessing and that men are making room for my gifts, huh? God had to keep bringing me back to get my blessing. I kept running, like Jonah. God told me that more people believe in me in Colorado than ever before. I plan to go back to my hometown to give because that is what we are to do, to sow back into others, but God told me that only when you are honored somewhere else are you honored in your hometown. "Truly I tell you," he continued, "no prophet is accepted in his hometown."

Luke 4:24 So we must be willing to go where God sends us. God sends his people out to other lands, foreign lands. I have come to love Denver and it's great. After 15 years, it is where I desire to be and build what God has called me to build, hmm? But it was hard at first, huh? I mean I was homeless here with my family because I chose to give up my drug life. After that I have worked all hours of the day and night, I've walked off jobs at some others, and even had my divorce here in Denver. I worked all those jobs for so many years, three jobs for 13 years because God told me that ain't nobody got what you got, let your gifts make room for you. So, God gave me this restaurant. I sure worked for it, but it was God who gave it to me. It's God's plan that I am here in Denver. It's God's plan, hmm?

It is important to heed the call of God when he speaks.

When God speaks, it is important to heed the call. Sometimes no one will understand, huh? But what is there to understand? For if God says it, then do it. Believe God people. Believe God. All that time I was waiting on my dream to come to reality, and it seemed too long. And now God is moving quick. And we have to be ready to move with Him, huh? God says that He comes like a thief in the night. "You know very well that the day of the LORD will come like a thief in the night." 1 Thesselonians 5:2

No one knows the time, the day or the hour that God will come or call us home. No one, hmm? None of us know, huh? But we know that we are to be ready. And we have to be ready to say yes when God calls us to His work too, huh? God will do the work to get us ready, now, but we have to have our heart ready to move! We are to anticipate a life that will be lived with God in the Kingdom. And God said he is building us mansions and that they will have many rooms, huh? Because there will be many people. He wants many in his kingdom. That is His heart's desire, huh? That many are saved or He wouldn't have sent Jesus. His love is fierce for us, yeah! His love is fierce! He never leaves us, huh? Never! We leave him, huh, but He never leaves us. Never! No. Jesus said, "My father's house has many rooms; if that were not so, would I have told you that I am going there to prepare a place for you?" John 14:2

So, we must care about the things of God. We must care about people. God told me I was the one chosen for this call, for this time and for the people. And the people are ready, huh? The people are excited! But God told me I was to love people and I was to do it through my cooking and through caring for people, huh? And I have always done that, since I was a little boy I was defending the weaker children. I was inviting people to my apartment and cooking for them to care for them. When I was in the streets, I was selling drugs to them and preaching the Word of God to them telling them about Jesus. Today God tells me to build his Kingdom, to raise and train the leaders, huh? That I am to train up the next generation of leaders for his kingdom. The time is now. God has made me a warrior. If I don't do it, huh? If we don't or won't do what God has called us to do before birth, hmm? God will find someone else to do it, because it's got to be done. It's got to be done! God told me to go to the churches and tell my story, that a lot will be saved unto the Kingdom by hearing what God did for me. He told me that the land that he is giving me to tell this story is the whole world. God's story and what He did for my life and how He turned it around and saved me, restored me and elevated me needs to be told to the whole world, huh? Because that's God, huh? Won't He do it, huh? Hmm?

God got everybody out of the way that could hinder His story. The story has got to be told. God told me: "Now is your season." We all have seasons and it is important to know what season you're in, hmm? Because if you don't know your season, you can be distracted and doing all kinds of things that could lead you away from your blessing. When God is raising you, you must walk out your blessing. I know this is my time for my blessing, Amen? This is my time, my season. God has said the first shall be last and the last shall be first, huh? Just do them no wrong. Just do the people no wrong. So, God will raise me up, huh? God will raise you up, huh? We don't have to fight for position, huh? God will do it!

God says for us to: "Stay the course because in due time, I will raise you among men to tell them about Me." Huh? "And whether you walk among kings or you walk among peasants, you will have favor. You will have favor because I go before you and I go behind you and I make a way in the desert, so walk with favor among the kings now. And tell them your story." Hmm? Because they have influence and they are leaders. See I know God favors me, huh? I know I am one of His that favor comes to, huh? He tells me and positions me to walk and talk among great men. But favor never comes without a price, huh? No. Favor never comes without a call of God, Hmm? Because He wants us to do something great for Him, huh? There is something that God wants me to do with that favor and something you are to do with your favor, huh? Your favor is for you and your blessing is for you, 'cause God wants to do something mighty with your life, Hmm? A life turned over to God is the greatest life you can live, hmm? Hmm? He wants me to tell my story. He wants me to share among men the greatness of God. He wants me to make His name great to the people. See favor comes with responsibility, hmm? Huge responsibility. I am responsible to tell the people about what God did for me and how He is real and will it do for them.

God tells me they will listen to me because he will make them hear me and receive me.

They will receive and hear me because God will make them listen to me. God told me that he will make men give unto my bosom. He will make them, not Mo. See, God is so amazing. He set it all up for me. He will set it all up for you too, in your season. If you don't get weary of doing good, he will establish you and set your feet up on a rock. See God's doing it His way. He is bringing the people to my doorstep at the restaurant that are responding and hearing His call and the call of what we are doing. They are compelled to give, to offer help because God is moving on their hearts.

I am always very real at the restaurant. I always say that I am like the barbershop in Sheridan. Because we keep it real. We talk about everything. One day, I had just gotten back to the restaurant and I was in the Spirit, huh? I was ministering to the people in the Spirit of the Holy Ghost, huh? And I mean the Spirit of God was powerful and we were having church. We were having church in the back of the restaurant. Six of us, two couples and I were having church. I started after telling them how hard it has been and how much of a struggle financially it has been. It was and still is a lot, huh? I mean we opened with no money and it takes a lot to keep a restaurant going. One year is a great accomplishment! So anyway, I was telling the customers the truth, shoot, I'm not gonna fake it! God said, "Tell them what you need." Now, I wasn't telling them for that reason, but I was being honest. I was telling them that I may have to close the restaurant. I don't want to, but I might have to. I owe everybody. Shoot, any day it could close down. Imagine living everyday with that pressure. This man said, "No, Mo don't close. We need you here! The food is too good and we need you!" He said, "Mo here is my number," and he handed me a paper. He said "Call me Mo if they're gonna shut you down. I'll lend you the money. Call me Mo." That man said he'd lend me the money, hmm? And people do this all the time!

Man, God is amazing. God doesn't want this to close. God does not want the restaurant to close. And I was close to giving it up after my year anniversary and after my book was published, to go on the road and just work for God. It's so hard and I am tired of the struggle. But God won't let it close, huh? Now God gave me a new vision for the time for it's a NEW time in the season of the LORD, oh come ON somebody! And I know what season I am in, huh, and what time it is now, huh? The time is now for me to keep pressing through, huh? The time is now because the blessing is here and it is my season, huh? See, you have to KNOW what season you're in, so that when the enemy comes and hard times come, you can speak to it and say, Get behind me oh Satan, huh? You will not take my blessing from me, huh? No, you will not. For if God is for you, then who can be against, GLORY TO GOD, PRAISE JESUS. The devil may try to lie, to deceive, to destroy, huh? But I was brought to this place, to THIS place for such a time as this! GLORY TO GOD, Oh, thank you LORD! Yes, LORD, I was brought to this place for a time like today! And men are going to make room for me 'cause I have something to say, huh? I'm going to tell them of the deliverance of Jesus. I'm going to tell them and ain't no one who can stop me now! No. LORD have mercy, yes JESUS, I hear and receive your call, mmm, I hear and accept your call on my life. I was born for such a time as this!

God's will and purpose will prevail. And I will miss what I could have had here. Now, I know that God can establish me anywhere and the things meant for me of God are for me only, huh? But what if this was what was meant for me and I am to travel and build God's kingdom? But see, I had to be sure, huh? We have to be sure about where we are supposed to be. So, we have to wait on God, huh? I had to be sure this is what God wants because it has been so hard. And we think it should be easy, hmm? But God says that it will be, for God says after you suffer a little while, I will establish you, huh? God says that men will make room for me, that my gifts will make room for me. We must operate in our gifts, church. And when we do, room will be made for us. God says that your gift will make room for you. "A man's gift makes room for him and brings him before the great." Proverbs 18:16

See, it is important to know your gifts. You must invest in your gift first and people might get mad that you are doing that. But you got to do it, huh? You've got to invest in your gifts, hmm? God has given me many gifts. My struggle was great, but my gifts from God are greater. And the struggle is what refined my gifts so that they could be used to the fullest and with the most power. If you know your gifts, then you are not detoured by the struggle, huh? My time is now. God has this for me. But that's not all God has for me.

This is not all God has for me, but God does have this for me.

This is not all God has for me, but God does have this for me. My time is now. The call on my life is so big, that I have to be in tune with Him to know where to move. So, God is keeping it moving at his pace, huh? He wants me to do both. To do the restaurant but to build His ministry and church. So, if God said it than I guess I can do it. Nothing is too hard for God. But one thing I KNOW, huh? You have a call on your life, hmm? You have things that only you can do, huh? What are your gifts, huh? Why are you not operating in your gifts? Your gifts will make room for you, man, and bring you among great men! You need to focus on your gifts first and then where God places you and what he brings you to, will be for you! You cannot give up during the hard times, for God is wanting to establish you! Ain't nobody can do it but God. All my 13 years of working three jobs, I never lost the vision God gave me, because I knew God's voice was real. What God has for you is for you and only you, huh! But you must work hard and not give up! He will do it! Man, He will do it! Don't give up because He is making your name great among men, huh! After you suffer for a little while, He will establish you! And after you trust Him in the place that He has placed you and walk forward in His appointment for you, you will see the deliverance of the LORD. And I know one thing, I was brought here for a time such as this...and so are you. Thank you, LORD. Praise you JESUS.

Some of you are in your season, huh? If you are in your season of anointing, God will 'cause you to have that anointing and a double anointing, hmm? Get ready, 'cause its fixin to happen when God overflows in your life, ain't no one, no thing, no person who can stop that flow, huh? Man, I'm telling you He is awesome! If you just don't give up! His love for you is fierce and what He has for you is overflow! Yeah, man! No one can do what God can do in your life! You were born for such a time as this! They can say what they wanna say, huh? All the haters, hmm? But it's yours! Claim your inheritance! Believe God! He loves you so much that He is comin' for you, huh? His love for you is fierce! His love is fierce!

"You did not choose Me but I chose you, and appointed you that you would go and bear fruit and that your fruit would remain so that whatever you ask of the Father in My name He may give you."

—John 15:16

Fierce

By Jesus Culture

Before I call
Before I ever cry
You answer me
From where the thunder hides
I can't outrun
This heart I'm tethered to
With every step
I collide with You

Like a tidal wave
Crashing over me
Rushing in to meet me here
Your love is fierce
Like a hurricane
That I can't escape
Tearing through the atmosphere
Your love is fierce

You cannot fail
The only thing I've found
That through it all
You've never let me down
You won't hold back
Relentless in pursuit
At every turn
I come face to face with you
Like a tidal wave

Crashing over me
Rushing in to meet me here
Your love is fierce
Like a hurricane
That I can't escape
Tearing through the atmosphere
Your love is fierce

You surround me
You chase me down
You seek me out
How could I be lost when you
have called me found?

You chase me down
You seek me out
How could I be lost when you
have called me found?

You chase me down
You seek me out
How could I be lost when you
have called me found?

Like a tidal wave
Crashing over me
Rushing in to meet me here
Your love is fierce

Like a hurricane
That I can't escape
Tearing through the atmosphere

His love is fierce
Your love is fierce
You never let go
Your love is fierce
Even now you surround me
Your love is fierce
Always, Always
His love is fierce
(Great is your love)
(Great is your love)
(It never fails)

Chapter 19

The Last Hour

Marriese's watch collection

"The desert and the parched land will be glad;
the wilderness will rejoice and blossom.
Like the crocus it will burst into bloom;
it will rejoice greatly and shout for joy...they will see the
glory of the LORD, the splendor of our God."
—Isaiah 35-1-2

And God told me He would show up in the last hour.

In the last hour God told me that He would show up. I had a storage unit. I had everything in there. Yes, everything was in there. I had my watch collection in there. Yeah man, I had a watch collection. And I had nice watches too. Shoot, I've been collecting watches for years. They were expensive watches. I let them all go. God told me to let them all go. And it didn't bother me, huh? No, it didn't bother me. God told me to let them all go, see? That was the past. God said to me to let it go. I feel so free.

For years, I was collecting those watches, from before I came to Denver until after I was still married. Now, I gave all of my possessions up when my wife and I came to Denver, when God told me to make a decision to choose either Him or the drug life. We gave it all up, but I kept my watches. I never gave those watches away even after all those years, until this year. And now God tells me to give them all away, hmm? He had told me to cut ties with me past, hmm? All the ties from my past life, hmm? In a way I was, yet the watches were the last little bit of what was holding me to the world, hmm? And I kept holding on, huh? I wouldn't let go of all of it, hmm? I mean I let go of some of it, huh? I let go of a lot, huh? But, God said that He was doing a new thing, hmm? Making a way in the desert, hmm? But that I would have to be ready for the new, hmm? And those watches represented the old way of life, hmm? From before the restaurant even, huh? From my old self, hmm? My carnal self, huh? When God wants to give me a new life, hmm? A new life in Him, huh? And I had to be willing to give up what I held in my past life, hmm, for God to give me the ways of him, huh? Huh? 'cause when we are in Christ, truly in Christ, the old is dead and the new has come, hmm? And God says don't look back but run towards the things of God.

When I was a little boy, my very first watch was a Micky Mouse watch with the black arms. I still remember it. I loved that watch, yeah. My dad bought me watches too, huh. Man, he bought me nice watches. He made sure I had everything nice. I didn't have any junk. He used to beat me though, if I didn't tell the time right with the black hands on my Mickey Mouse watch. I guess he wanted to make sure I knew how to tell time. Yeah, but when God tells me to go, huh, I don't look

back. I keep it moving. I don't look back. I'm like that.
I'm like that with relationships, with work, I just keep it
moving. I don't look back. Maybe I don't have a problem
keepin it moving because we moved around so much
as a child. We moved ten times in one year when I was
with my mama. That was hard, yeah. As a kid? Yeah, that
was hard. So now, watch this, God tells me I'm going to
be given a city, huh? That he is going to give me a city and
make my name great among men. This is what God tells
me. So, he's breaking me of my desire to run and move
and he is promising to give me a city. And then God gives
me visions of travel and moving our ministry worldwide.
So now, I get to see that I get to go, huh, but my home
base will always be Denver. See, I think it's one way, but
it's a different way completely with God. He heals us and
gives us more than we could ever want or desire. So, I
got to go, and I got to stay! But, it's God's way this time.
It's not Mo's way, huh? It's God's way and it's God's time,
huh? And as long as I do God's way, its Mo's way huh?
'cause my way is God's way now, hmm? I'm good, hmm?
It don't even matter what it is, huh? I'm good.

I have to give up my watches and trust His time.
Trust His time for my life. And although I give up my
watches, God is my timing and my source and He reveals
the next step to me. He says that I will see Him in the
last hour. He says tell the people: "They will see Me
(God) in the last hour." See, when I let go of my watches
and my attachment to things and my way, will I see God
in a way I never had before. Things become clearer. God
is always showing us more of him. Never do I have it
all. So, after I give up my earthly understanding of what
can be, will I see what I thought I could not. Man, God
is showing me some things! And those watches? And
who knew that all the years of collecting those watches

would someday have even a greater meaning on the day that my daddy told me to lay them down, huh? That to lay them down I will see more of Him, hmm? That to be called into the army of the LORD GOD, I must lay down my timing, my expectations, my everything, hmm? That it is when my greatest Apostolic calling will be revealed, huh? When I lay it down for the King of GLORY, huh? The King of Glory! GLORY TO GOD. In Isaiah 6:1 it says, "In the year King Uzziah died, I saw the LORD, high and exalted, seated on a throne." Here God called the boy Isaiah to be a prophet. When the King died, the boy Isaiah saw the LORD. But only after the thing (person) he kept in front of God was removed. Because God will have no other before Him. God will have no one taking his GLORY. After I gave up my hold on all of my past, God spoke about my future, hmm? After I let go of the fact that my wife remarried, huh? God called me as a pastor, hmm? I let her go, hmm? And I felt so free, huh? I let go of my past, huh? And God said now see me, hmm? For I am doing a new thing, Hmm? And eyes have not seen and ears have not heard, huh, what I the LORD will do for those who love me, huh?

"I waited patiently for the LORD; He turned to me and heard my cry. He lifted me out of the slimy pit, out of the mud and the mire; He set my feet on a rock and gave me a firm place to stand. He put a new song in my mouth, a hymn of praise to our God. Many will see and fear the LORD and put their trust in Him. Blessed is the one who trusts in the LORD, who does not look to the proud, to those who turn aside to false gods. Many, LORD my God are the wonders you have done, the things you have planned for us. No one can compare with you; were I to speak and tell of your deeds, they would be too many to declare." Psalm 40: 1-5.

I have been fighting it for years. Running from it. I said, no. I don't want to be a pastor, God. I don't want a church. I have been hurt by the church. I don't even call myself a Christian sometimes, but a follower of Jesus, because I have been so hurt. But God said, "It is time. The time is now. You will see me in the last hour and the time is now. It cannot wait. I am giving you a church." The last hour and seeing God in it is the most exciting to me. Nothing else matters. In writing this book, God is healing me of my past. God restores all my time lost, all my broken dreams, all my lost hopes. He does. Not me. Not Mo. So, let it all go and watch me, for God says, "I make all things new."

Only after all was removed, does God speak directly to me for my final calling. And God tells me that I will see Him in the last hour. He tells me the people will see Him in the last hour. This year, I gave up all my watches. Really, what God is saying is don't look back, huh? I am freeing you from your past and don't look back, huh? Jesus! Praise God! Don't you look back now, because I am doing a new thing, huh? Oh, come on somebody! Thank you, LORD. I am doing a new thing now, but whoa don't you look back to the thing that was before now, because if you look back in the last hour? Praise you Jesus, GLORY TO GOD. If you look back in the last hour, you won't see me, huh? If you LOOK BACK in that last hour, son, you won't see ME! Come on! And I am doing a NEW THING! If you look back? You become like Lot's wife and turn to stone, (salt). Jesus said it, that we must not look back. "No one who puts a hand to the plow and looks back is fit for the service in the Kingdom of God." Luke 9:62. I must move into what God has for me. God tells me that signs and wonders will follow. I am doing a new thing. Unless I am new, I cannot move into what God has for me. You cannot take old wineskins for new wine. "Neither do people pour new wine into old wineskins. If they do, the skins will burst; the wine will run out and the wineskins will be ruined. No, they pour new wine into new wineskins, and both are preserved." Matthew 9:17

Last year God had me living in a shed, huh? I am building my dream and I am living in a shed. Is that crazy? So many people had their foot on my neck. It was so heavy, I'm telling you. But God was freeing me. God was stripping me of all that I thought I needed but Him. God was showing me my dream in my hand and releasing me of all that I needed releasing from. Some that I messed up myself and some that had me tied and bound still to the damages and hurt from my past. And it was painful! I was in pain! I cried out to God on my face so many times at the restaurant, I was like God! Why are you doing this to me, huh? I was used to nice things and having a job! Now, I had no job and I was living with my friend Rusty in his shed. I mean I was grateful! Boy, that man was a blessing to me! He was my river in a dry land so many times, but it still was a desert! It still was a shed, huh? It wasn't what I was accustomed to in my years with my wife, in our later years. We had built a nice life and now here I was, with my dream in my hand and in the worst place financially that I had ever been in. I lost my car, huh? It was stolen while I was visiting my sick mama in Florida. Those people stole my car. I kept telling my friend it was there and when I got back to Denver to look for my car, it was not there. Man, I'm telling you I went through some stuff! I almost decided to go and leave Denver and that was three months before the restaurant opened. I was so tired of it. I thought this is too much for me. I had worked all year on my restaurant. I was tired. I was overwhelmed. I just got back from my mama being sick and now this? Man, I'm gone. You can have it, my restaurant, my dream and Denver. I. Am. Gone. But God said, Not this time, son. This is not the time to go, huh? God said, if you will turn to Me and trust in Me, I will make all things new. So, I began to walk everyday a mile to the restaurant, which needed so much work and I had no money. I borrowed cars here and there to get around, but I walked every day to that restaurant and I would praise God on the way there and I would praise God on the way back, huh? And I held my head up high and let no one get me down. But while I was there at the restaurant during those days? Man, I cried out to God literally and prayed and wept and fasted. And look what God did, boy. God made a way, hmm. God made a way through the desert when there was no way. But I had to be stripped and broken down to be raised up. I had to be humbled again! And I still would not be broken down as much as God would take me in the next year that the restaurant was opened, but God was showing me that I could rely on Him and He was going to complete what He started. He was going to make time restored for me. And then it wouldn't be until later on that God reminded me of the watches that were in my storage unit after He had told me to let it all go. Now I understand, those watches had to go too. Hard as it was, God was all the telling of time I needed. Because He would direct the timing. His timing is perfect, huh? His time is all that matters. On his watch, oh praise God, we should base our actions. Human time means nothing to God. He lives outside of our human constructed time. He is not bound by it nor limited of it. And neither are we when we live by God's time. Those watches, huh? God shows me that nothing compares to God's timing.

He determines what time is and how much time we have. And He can restore time lost, huh? He can restore and give back time to any situation. All the time you think you lost waiting on God? He can give you back 100-fold. Oh, come on somebody! Look and see what God is doing! He makes all things new in the last hour. And when God shows up, hmm? Everything changes! God told me to let those watches go! Finally let them go! Tell time now by Me. I am your source. I am your time and you will see Me in the last hour. We have to let go of all that we are to get to where God would have us to be. When God finally takes me to my Promised Land. I need no other time but His. Because He IS time, huh? He is time.

I was holding on, but no more! I am holding onto nothing more than Jesus. For if I hold on, I will not see God in the final hour. That's deep, man. When God shows up, EVERYTHING changes. And I will see Him in the last hour. This is what He is telling me. That the time is now. The people are ready to be freed of bondage and free of what is weighing them down. "The Spirit of the LORD is on me, because the LORD has anointed me to proclaim good news to the poor. He has sent me to bind up the brokenhearted, to proclaim freedom for the captives and release from darkness for the prisoners." Isaiah 61:1 God showing up is powerful.

God changes everything. He changes entire situations. He restores what is lost and broken when we focus on Him. When we leave behind what God tells us to leave behind, He will restore what we thought was lost forever. What we need most. What is best for us, what we were created to be and what is best for living out our calling, our purpose, our reason for being here. And who better to do it than the one who knew why He made us. "They will see me in the last hour." In Isaiah 35:1-2, God is sought after and longed for in the darkest hour. When he shows up, it is like a hero walking onto a scene. He is their water in a dry desert. Dead things come to life again when God shows up. In the last hour, God is all we need. God is the one thing of anything we do need in our last hour, in our worst hour, in our most desperate hour. That is the only thing I needed in my divorce season, in my stripping season and in my building the restaurant season. It is like an anticipation when we wait on God! It is like a long-awaited relief. Because we know when He shows up, all is going to be made right. We know when God comes, Lazarus will walk again! And we wait on God to do it. God can make our dead places come to life again, hallelujah! God can do it! Come now, one and all and see the GLORY of the LORD. And He will do it, huh?

I feel in control now, yet my extreme helplessness of my childhood situations tried to lodge a permanent place in my soul, but God wouldn't let that take hold, huh? God says that they will see Me in the last hour! I believe that the call is now; that the people have to get ready. God is moving and this is my most important time of my life now. God would not have cleaned me, restored me and called me if the battle was not significant. God tells us to seek no one but Him and He will bring all things to us. God tells us seek Me and I will bring the victory. And they will see Me in the last hour.

"Be strong and do not fear; your God will come, he will come with a vengeance; with divine retribution, he will come to save you."

—Isaiah 35:3-4

Chapter 20

Not for My Glory but Yours

"Because you are his sons,
God sent his Spirit who calls out Abba Father."
—Galations 4:6

God told me that people are going to know Him through me.

It is a calling. Through me people are going to know Him. God has called me to build his people. Jesus has called me. My mind is made up. I will serve the people. I go to Denver City Park every Sunday to hand out information about the restaurant and the nonprofit. People call me Daddy Bruce. Can you believe it, huh? And I love him and what he did. I am in my element here too, on the streets with the people, just like in the kitchen. Maybe even more. When I first came to Denver, that is what God had me do. He gave me a job and paid me for it and let me be two years on the streets

145

of Denver, so I could know Denver like I knew Miami. But I wasn't selling drugs this time. This time I was doing things legit. For two years, God paid me while I was building my ministry. And everyone loved me and trusted me. The hardest thing with those on the streets is trust. I used to sometimes take them to the liquor store and give them a few bucks to buy beer. You know? They trusted me and I could show them the love. Just like my grandmother did when she picked her children up off the street, took them home, fed and cleaned them, gave them money and dropped them back off on the street. I have a great love for people where they are at. That's how Jesus tells me to love. I am comfortable on the streets and I always knew my church would be on the streets.

I hear God every day. He is with me all day long, talking to me and I am listening. When you hear the Holy Ghost and know His voice, you understand that what Jesus says is real, is genuine reality, and you learn to walk in what He says. Jesus never said Lazarus was dead, huh? He never said he was dead. He said he was sleeping. We said he was dead. The ways of God are genuine reality and when we learn that, our whole world changes. Because God's ways are real. And He will do what only He can in our lives. So, I don't stress, hmm? Because I know that whatever God does, it will be for my good. So, we have to hear Him, huh? That is how I live my life. That is how I hear the things of God. That is how I act as a Prophet of the Living God. That is how I know to move in the direction that He tells me to move. Without God, hmm...without God, huh? There will be times where people will not understand how I change direction or the things I do. But I am listening to God all day and he is speaking to me all day. I listen all day long.

On July 19, 2017, I almost lost my dream. I almost lost my entire building of the restaurant. We were three weeks out from my one-year anniversary celebration and I was driving my van to go get food and supplies for the restaurant like I do every morning. On my way back to the restaurant, I meant to stop and get gas, even hit my brakes to turn in the gas station but God told me to keep going. Well, as I drove up on the restaurant, I noticed a City of Denver firetruck on the highway next to our building on the far side of the restaurant just as I was driving up on my side of it. I noticed that the firetruck had slowed way down and the firemen were staring at my building. I couldn't see what they were looking at but I did see smoke which looked like my cook had lit the smoker. As I was on the phone with my friend I pulled around the side of the building that the firetruck had been looking at and saw that the building had caught fire. "Oh my God", I shouted, "we're on fire"! I jumped out of the running van and ran inside to tell my staff, grabbed a fire extinguisher and put that fire out! It was large and had almost reached the roof shingles. With seconds lapsing only, the firetruck was there and four firemen had jumped out! They couldn't believe I had put it out but they followed after me. A spare door that had been stored on the side where the fire was and that door was halfway burned to ashes. The entire side of the wood building was black. Two more minutes and the fire would have reached the roof shingles and the building would have been engulfed. My staff had been in and out all morning and no one saw it. God had it for me to be the one to see and to witness his power, Glory to God. What are the chances that a firetruck would be going by exactly at the time that the fire erupted. Exactly at the time? Boy, if that ain't God. He told me to go on to the restaurant! And I drove up just in time. Just in time. And I had just decided to serve God and build a church in the same block as the restaurant. Boy, the devil is so mad! The devil has never left me alone! Never! But the devil is a liar and what God does for me, boy! What God does for me!

I need to teach people how to walk in the spirit. I shift into the spirit often. I must teach people how to hear Him. But when we hear His voice we need to obey. He changes our reality. Man, does He! He does what only He can do. We have to use blinders and learn the Spirit realm. God's voice to me is my greatest gift. The Spirit of God is our greatest treasure. We need to hear with our hearts because He is always talking to us. My whole life God, has told me things before they have happened. People may say that God tells them things but I know for sure what God tells me, hmm. Because I hear His voice and I have learned to hear His voice. And what He tells me is awesome! We must learn to operate in the spirit which is our heart. God told me to think about new beginnings because everything is done different now. I am on a new path and every day is hard. But when I hear God and go where He tells me to go, I'm good. I want only what God wants. God do what only you can do. This is how I live every day. The Spirit of the Living God is my greatest treasure.

My light is no longer hiding under the bush. God told me He is going to use me and they will see the burning bush-its heavy-ain't no one going to stop me.

No one is gonna stop me, they will see the burning bush. God is using me and my light is no longer hiding under the bush. I know now the fire was for me to see. The devil may have planned it, but not before God already knew about it, Glory to God. Praise you Jesus. The devil may have started it, Glory to God, but God finished it. And mine eyes have seen the coming of the Lord. That fire was for me and God, because God just got done telling me that my light cannot be hidden under a bush any longer. Glory to God. Let it roar. No longer will God let me suffer by not following my calling. That represents the fire people are going to see. The power of God is so great in my life, that people can't help but see it. That "burning bush" today had meaning! Praise God! It was God's confirmation call to me to lead the people and make Him known among the people. That was my burning bush and for it to be like the burning bush Moses saw. God was in the middle of Moses' burning bush and God is present in mine. God had to be in the midst of it. He HAD to be there. Just like God had to be there today and it was all okay. It was meant for God and I. It burned but like when Moses saw the fire in the bush, that fire miraculously did not burn up the bush. My fire miraculously did not burn up the building. So not only did God save us, He is too powerful to just be reactive. He planned for He and me to see it. I saw God's power today, huh? It was powerful. God was there with me and spoke to me about the seriousness of my calling and what He now wants me to do. He controls my future. Whatever He wants, I want. My burning bush today initiated my calling and God's timing. The time is now. The warrior must advance when the King commands. That burning bush was God's promise to me today that He is with me in my call and He goes before me. That burning bush will be an image I always remember of what the restaurant must be, a beacon of hope and love to the people. God specifically spoke to me about my call and my light not hiding anymore. God told time of the burning bush ahead of time, to when an attack came on me, it was used for good and not evil like it was planned to do. Glory to God. What a treasure is the Spirit of God.

I told God that if He would let me hear Him that I wouldn't make any decision and I would wait on Him.

I would wait on Him and not make any decision if He would let me hear Him. The Spirit realm is heavy and we have to learn to wait on God and hear His directions. He does new things and makes all things new. He can change our world, our reality and us in an instant. One touch of Jesus' robe is all we need and we are healed, our reality is forever changed. I told God that I did not want to see or hear Him through anybody. I just wanted Him. When we seek Him with all our hearts, He will come to us. "You will seek Me and find Me when you seek Me with all of your heart." Jeremiah 29:13. God told me I keep on running from Him. Even after all He has done from me, I rebel. It is known that the Prophets of God rebel. That is because the calling is so heavy. I can defienetly say that I have experienced both, walking with God and rebelling. God told me that He was making me a pastor. What God begins He will finish, I am confident of this. Just look at the restaurant. I worked for it but it was God who gave it to me. It is God who keeps it every day. Look at what He has delivered me from throughout my entire life. I have heard His voice and I will let no one distract me. God is bringing about into my life a reconciling 100 times more than what was taken from me. God said, "If you are faithful for a little while then I will steady you and resestablish you." God said that. And he said that HE will be the one to resestablish me. Not Mo, not anyone but Him. Because it is for God's glory. God says that He will do it. We are not to worry, we are to focus on Him and He will bring the victory! This life was so hard. Especially as a little boy. As an adult I wanted to give up and kill myself so many times. But as the song by Teddy Pendergrass said, "It don't hurt anymore." I have never known anyone like Jesus. He comforts. He is the great comforter. This doesn't mean that I don't struggle, or get mad. It means that I don't worry anymore. I don't worry about anything because God is real and He has this. He has me, hmm? Whatever happens, I'm good with it, huh? And when you live that way, you are free. Jesus said the Son comes so that He will make you free and free we are indeed. I feel so light. I have let go of so much that has been weighing me down. There is no life like a freedom and a life in Jesus. While God is doing a whole makeover in me, He promises me that He will make those that stole from me give it back a 100 fold. God 'caused people to give unto their bosom. God told me that if go any other way then the way he was telling me to go, then people will not receive me but judge me for your past. He encouraged me to not worry because I will get paid for your past 100 x 100. God sent me to be a pastor, hmm. That is where my heart is at and because it is God's path and God spoke to me, that is where my blessing will be. See, what God has for you is for you. But you must hear Him, wait on Him and then do what He says. And this is all for God's GLORY. Who would have thought that God could take a thug and establish him and make him a pastor, Huh? Who could have written that story? Man, no one but God! No one but Jesus. No one but the Living God!

And when God establishes you, no one, not anyone, can take it away from you, huh? And the people who wouldn't support you, huh? Well they are going to have to support you know 'cause God will make them. He will change their hearts, you don't have to do it, huh? He will do it! He will do it all. And the love that was missing from my life as a child, huh? Well, now the people I serve give me the love. And the love I get from God is like a river and overflows in my life so it pours out to others so I don't even notice if I'm not getting the love because God loves me and it's enough for me. No one, nobody can "out give" God. No one can "out love" God. All my tears, all my tears He kept and collected and now his mighty river pours forth in my life and from my life. Praise Jesus. And baby, it don't hurt now, huh? It don't hurt now.

GLORY TO GOD.

"These things are the things
God has revealed to us by his Spirit.
The Spirit searches all things,
even the deep things of God."
—1 Corinthians 2: 10

Spirit of the Living God
Meredith Andrews

Spirit of the Living God
Spirit of the Living God
We only wanna hear your voice
Were hanging on every word.
Spirit of the Living God
Spirit of the Living God
We wanna know you more and more
Were hanging on every word
Speak to us
Spirit of the Living God
Spirit of the Living God
We're leaning into all you are
Everything else can wait
Spirit of the Living God
Spirit of the Living God
Come now and breathe upon our hearts
Come now and have Your way
'cause when You speak
When You move
When You do what only You can do
It changes us, it changes what we see
And what we seek
When You come in the room
When You do what only You can do
It changes us, it changes what we see
And what we seek
You're changing everything
Spirit of the Living God

Spirit of the Living God
Come now and breathe upon our hearts
Come now and have your way
When You speak and when You move
When You do what only You can do
It changes us, it changes what we see
And what we seek
When You come in the room
When You do what only You can do
It changes us, it changes what we see
And what we seek
You're changing everything
When You move
You move all our fears
When You move
You move us to tears
When You move
You move all our fears
When You move
You move us to Tears
When You fall
We fall on our knees
When You fall
We fall at Your feet
When You fall
We fall on our knees
When You fall
We fall at Your feet
Yeah
When You speak
When You move

When You do what only You can do
It changes us, it changes what we see
And what we seek
When You come in the room
When You do what only You can do
It changes us, it changes what we see
And what we seek
You're changing everything!
"With zeal have I been zealous for the LORD
God of Hosts"
When You fall
We fall at Your feet
When You fall
We fall on our knees
When You fall
We fall at Your feet
Yeah
When You speak
When You move
When You do what only You can do
It changes us, it changes what we see
And what we seek
When You come in the room
When You do what only You can do
It changes us, it changes what we see
And what we seek
You're changing everything!

"With zeal have I been zealous for the LORD
God of Hosts"

—St. Teresa

Epilogue

I have learned throughout my journey that it is important to live life and not let life live you. So many people don't understand this.

I am a Chef and I own a restaurant called Anointed BBQ & Soul Food, or better known as "Anointed."

I feed the people on a regular basis.

I am Prophet of God and
was called by God as a young man.

I feed the souls of people daily.

These are my passions,
my gifts and my callings by the LORD.

I know that these stories have fed your Soul.

GLORY TO GOD

Life happens. And yes, we all have choices. But sometimes we must accept what we cannot change. There are all sorts of quotes about this and scriptures too, but this is what God gave me. To live your life and to live life to the fullest, we must understand what that means. I believe that it means you **keep it moving**. Accept what you cannot change and just **keep it moving, yeah.**

This book is just one of many that God has told me to write. This book is my first. It will just scratch the surface of what God has given me for you.

This book is a collection of my stories. Hopefully these stories will begin to paint a picture with words that describe who God is to me and what God has brought me through.

So, in a way, this book is really about God, huh? Because you cannot read my story or see my life and not see God. He lives on every page of this book.

Before God gave me **Anointed BBQ & Soul Food** He gave me **Hedges and Highway Outreach Ministries**. That is really where my heart is, in my non-profit. I love giving people food but it's more important for the spiritual food to be given.

To tell them who God is.

The title of this book, "*40 Years in the Wilderness: The Making of a Man*" describes perfectly what God did with me. The Israelites had 40 years of wandering in their way out of bondage from Egypt. The Israelites were chosen of God for a purpose. God could have chosen any people group just like He can choose any person He wants, because He is God. God chose the Israelites to be a witness to the world. And this choosing would come with a cost and a training in the ways of the LORD. Before the Israelites could attain their Promised Land, they had to know God, huh? They had to know His voice and know He was faithful, huh? God had to be certain that He could trust them and that they would follow His ways.

Just as God chose the Israelites, He has chosen me too and from a very early age, to be His mouthpiece and His prophet. He has had His hand on my life since a baby. He chose me for a purpose and I believe that is in my calling to tell the people about the faithfulness of God. I have lived it! I know without a doubt that God is real.

However, this "choosing" does not come without a cost. God chose me and gave me 40 years of HIS training and pressing to make me into the man I am today. God provided for me daily and I have learned to trust Him in the deserts of my life. God taught me to never give up.

Never give up.

Your life has meaning.

What God has for you is for YOU!

You have a Promised Land.

But as Jesus said,
you must give up your life to find your life.

With God ALL things are possible.

This is my story and my life and I rejoice and thank God for saving me and rescuing me; for choosing me and stripping me to make me new for Him, for it made me into the warrior that I am today.

Now he leads me into the Promised Land.
And he will lead you too.

GLORY TO GOD.

So Let's Keep it Moving!

"Whoever finds their life will lose it,
and whoever loses their life for my sake will find it."
Spoken By Jesus

—Matthew10:39

The Calling

Isaiah 61

"The Spirit of the Sovereign LORD is on me,
because the LORD has anointed me
to proclaim the good news to the poor.
He has sent me to bind up the brokenhearted,
to proclaim freedom for the prisoners."

Heeding the Call of God

Isaiah 6:1

Isaiah 61

Marriese at his Nov 2017 Neighborhood Outreach Event

Marriese Jones, Sr.

November 2017

Anointed BBQ & Soul Food

Mo's Flagship Restaurant Opened August 4, 2016

164

Anointed BBQ & Soul Food, Sheridan Colorado:
first Year in Business 2016-2017

H & H Outreach's first Hog Roast: May 2017

Anointed's Famous Rib Dinner
Creamy Mac N Cheese and Collard Greens

Pulled Pork, Black Eyed Peas & Collards

166

Solomon '"Boy" and Maggie Jones

Maggie Lee Jones

168

Mo cooking at his restaurant, 2017

Marriesa "Chonna"
(Marriese's eldest daughter)

Marriesa & Dean working at Anointed BBQ

Mo greeting an old coworker
at Anointed

Mo at his smoker at Anointed

Mo and his son Marriese Jr.
at the 2017 December Outreach

December 2017
Toy Give-Away Event

Mo giving an interview to FOX NEWS

*One year later Mo at his second Annual Neighborhood Outreach Day
cutting the H & H Cake 2017*

Maggie Lee Jones   Marriese "Mo" Jones

WELCOME TO ANOINTED BBQ & SOUL FOOD

Anointed BBQ & Soul Food is an authentic soul food restaurant that will take you on a culinary explosion of flavor every time you dine! Founded in 2016 by Marriese "Mo" Jones, **Anointed** specializes in southern cuisine prepared fresh daily. **Anointed Chef Mo** shares with the world his love and passion of cooking, never forgetting the responsibility that his grandmother, **Maggie Jones** passed onto him, to care for others.

The young Mo learned to cook from his grandmother in her kitchen in a small town in Miami, Fla. Continuing now with her legacy, Mo treats every guest in his restaurant just like his grandmother did when they entered her home and were in need of love, care and family. Mo serves up food and love to nourish the **BODY & the SOUL** when guests enter **Anointed**. However, to know something of Mo, you must first learn something of the legendary **Maggie Jones**.

Maggie Jones was born in 1925 in Alabama. During her life she took great pride in her vocation as a laborer and housewife. Married to her soulmate "Boy" Jones, together they worked and raised a family in Southern Alabama and eventually settled in South Florida. Her care for others was common talk among all and Mo tells a story of how one morning, as a teenager, he awoke only to find that his grandmother had given away his brand -new shoes to a homeless man. As Mo was upset, Maggie instructed him that this man had no shoes and he had many to spare! Maggie loved her family unconditionally and welcomed everyone regardless of race, color or creed. As the matriarch of a family of 17 children, she instilled values of a strong work ethic, yet cared for the small details of life, like making sure to have Mo's favorite cornbread ready for him every day after school. Maggie's 47 Grandchildren, 111 Great Grandchildren, 99 Great, Great Grandchildren attest mostly to her great LOVE. Mo's tribute to Maggie lives on in the food you're eating! Mo was given a vision of owning his own restaurant "**Anointed BBQ & Soul Food**" in 2003. Working 3 jobs for 13 years, Mo never gave up on his dream, passion & calling!

Welcome...Enjoy & Come Back Soon!!

Anointed BBQ & Soul Food

2504 WEST HAMDEN AVENUE

SHERIDAN, CO 80110

303-781-5565

WWW.ANOINTEDBBQ.COM

Hours:

Monday-CLOSED

Tuesday - Thursday 11AM-8PM

Friday-Saturday 11 AM-Late Hours

Sunday 11 AM-5PM

The Anointed BBQ Menu

172

*Anointed's first November
Neighborhood Outreach Day 2016*

*Mo Serving Homeless Teens
with H & H and Urban Park*

*Kids and Parents
December 2017 Outreach*

H & H Stockings for Homeless

Mo speaking at his first event at Anointed

Mo & Grill Master Cousin Tommy

Car Give Away
November 2016

Mo and his beautiful daughter Chonna
and H & H Outreach Worker Mary Ellen
feeding homeless youths.

Anointed's first Neighborhood
OutreachNovember 2016

Mo promoting his One Year Anniversary
at Anointed BBQ & Soul Food

176

Voice of the Rocky Mountain Empire

THE DENVER POST

THURSDAY, NOVEMBER 27, 2008 · MOSTLY CLOUDY ▲ 40° ▼ 21° ■16B · DENVERPOST.COM · ©THE DENVER POST · 50 CENTS PRICE MAY VARY OUTSIDE METRO DENVER ✴✴

...SGIVING ›› Chef's labor a gift to those "in the wilderness"

Denver Rescue Mission chef Marriese Jones has known addiction and homelessness — and how to fight it. RJ Sangosti, The Denver Post

A generous helping of healing

By Colleen O'Connor The Denver Post

Chaos reigned just 15 minutes before the end of the Great Thanksgiving Banquet at the Denver Rescue Mission, when one of the servers shouted over her shoulder that they needed more turkey.

Chef Marriese Jones whipped his head around, looking for turkey. He'd cooked 50. They couldn't be all gone.

Turns out one of the cooks had forgotten to put more trays of turkey into the oven to heat.

"I left the kitchen and this is what I get?" said Jones, only half-joking with his staff.

A cook rushed to get tinfoil to cover the turkey. But he pulled up short at the rack, which was suddenly empty of all foil.

"Where did it go?" he said.

"I messed it over there," said Jones, jabbing a finger toward the back.

He had tried to warn volunteers against handing out pieces of foil to the diners, who kept requesting doggie bags, which are not allowed. But every time Jones turned his back, to stir gravy or dish up cranberry sauce, volunteers would dish up more turkey ... on, great handfuls of foil and head back out.

Denver Rescue Mission ›› A thousand pounds of turkey prepared. »21A

Travel ›› Interstate 70 traffic expected to be lighter than usual. »1B

Football ›› Previews of the NFL games. »1C

LH57 » 20A

dp **Video** ›› See chef Marriese Jones as he works at the Denver Rescue Mission. »denverpost.com

Above: Jones greets grateful diners at Wednesday's meal at the mission at 1130 Park Avenue West. RJ Sangosti, The Denver Post

Blessing of leftovers visits rescue mission

By Sally S. Ho
The Denver Post

dp **Poll** ›› Do you have more to be thankful for this Thanksgiving compared with last?
»denverpost.com

They had 1,000 pounds of turkey prepared, but the Denver Rescue Mission served only about half of it at this year's Great Thanksgiving Banquet, get underway Wednesday.

The mission had prepared 1,000 meals based on the flagging economy. Now it has 500 meals worth of leftovers that can be used throughout the weekend, according to Greta Walden, a spokeswoman for the mission.

Brad Meuli, president of the mission, noted the lively, saying that although the need is there although the number of people coming in was about the same as last year.

"Mostly single men served us, on normal hour of folks," Meuli said. Overall, "we've served 10,000 more meals this year, so I'm a little surprised there are not more families here."

Among those few families was the Angulo clan.

Recently separated from his wife, Ray Angulo is homeless in Denver and wanted a Thanksgiving meal.

He brought his five children for their first experience at the Denver Rescue Mission.

"There's nothing wrong with it. Everyone struggles. I in fact going a hard time too," Angulo said. "But I also wanted these brave and know how things are in the real world, that this could happen."

Once again, the mission offered free long-distance phone calls courtesy of Qwest, so folks could reconnect with loved ones.

"Usually we are about seeing people on Thanksgiving," said Mark Mulligan, of Qwest. "Sometimes that phone call just stretches the flag for them."

New Jobs Raises free the call, and most of the diners called on such as Mayor John Hickenlooper and Denver City Council members.

Now in his sixth year, the mission banquet for the homeless they prepared 600 pounds of stuffing, 400 pounds of sweet potatoes, 600 pounds of mixed gravy and cheese, and 600 servings of three kinds of pies.

Sally S. Ho: 303-954-1638 or sho@denverpost.com

The Anointed Story...

A tribute to Grandma Maggie

The stories that I have told you have given you just a glimpse of what God has brought me through. I learned to cook just like my grandmother and that is how **Anointed BBQ & Soul Food Restaurant** (better known as "**Anointed**") was formed. Just like no one ever left Grandmother's house hungry, that is how it is at **Anointed**. We feed people's souls and their bodies. The food is anointed and it is anointed with love! That is why people come back over and over again. I mean the food is great, but it is the love that people are craving in today's world. **Anointed** is like a house, actually it is like Grandmother's house. It is not very big, sometimes you have to cram yourself in, just as if you were at grandmother's house with all of the family. We all crammed in for good food, laughter and love. That is want I give people today at **Anointed**.

Welcome To Anointed BBQ & Soul Food

Anointed BBQ & Soul Food is an authentic soul food restaurant that will take you on a culinary explosion of flavor every time you dine! Founded in 2016 by Marriese "Mo" Jones, Anointed specializes in southern cuisine prepared fresh daily. Anointed Chef Mo shares with the world his love and passion of cooking, never forgetting the responsibility that his grandmother, Maggie Jones passed onto him..to care for others. The young Marriese learned to cook from his grandmother in her kitchen in a small town in Miami, Fla. Continuing on now with her legacy, Mo treats every guest in his restaurant just like his grandmother did when they entered her home and were in need of love, care and family. Mo serves up food and love to nourish the BODY & the SOUL when guests enter Anointed. However, to know something of Mo, you must first learn something of the legendary Maggie Jones. Maggie Jones was born in 1925 in Alabama. During her life she took great pride in her vocation as a laborer and housewife. Married to her soulmate "Boy" Jones, together they worked and raised a family in Southern Alabama and eventually settled in South Florida. Her care for others was common talk among all and Mo tells a story of how one morning, as a teenager, he awoke only to find that his grandmother had given away his brand -new shoes to a homeless man. As Marriese was upset, Maggie instructed him that this man had no shoes and he had many to spare! Maggie loved her family unconditionally and welcomed everyone regardless of race, color or creed. As the matriarch of a family of 17 children, she instilled values of a strong work ethic, yet cared for the small details of life, like making sure to have Marriese's favorite cornbread ready for him every day after school. Maggie's 47 grandchildren, 111 great-grandchildren, 99 great, great-grandchildren attest mostly to her great LOVE. Mo's tribute to Maggie lives on in the food you're eating! Marriese was given a vision of owning his own restaurant "Anointed BBQ & Soul Food" in 2003. Working three jobs for 13 years, Mo never gave up on his dream, passion & calling! Welcome... Enjoy & Come Back Soon!!

Anointed Customer Comments...

What Denver Foodies are saying about Anointed...

7/13/2017 "My wife and I had enjoyed this food recently and we were impressed! Wow! This is some of the best southern food in the Denver Metro area. The hospitality is that of a family dinner which is great! The flavor combinations in the dishes are fantastic. A great mixture of spicy, smokey, sweet, and savory in the dishes. The ribs are cooked to perfection and the barbecue sauce is excellent! Also try the potato salad and baked beans for sides you will not be disappointed. We look forward to going back!!"

7/13/2017 "If you haven't eaten here yet, something is wrong with you. OMG Mr. Mo has pleased my southern stomach. This is some of the best food I've had since living here. Thanks Mr. Mo."

6/17/2017 "I haven't even tasted the food yet but the vibe in here is great. Feels like you are home. I know the food will be great. Will update soon"

6/14/2017 Last night a group of my friends and I went to Anointed BBQ for my friend's birthday. This place far exceeded all expectations!!! Mo, who owns the restaurant, was absolutely amazing! He was surprised to see 20 people coming in all at once, and when we told him we were celebrating a birthday he was so honored. He even offered us free drinks and cake!! He was beyond kind!

6/14/2017 "Hands down, this is the best southern food in all of Denver. We walked in last night with a group of about 20 for a birthday party. Most places would be stressed to have such a large group arrive, but the owner Mo welcomed us with open arms. Mo spent some time sharing his story with us, which was such a blessing to hear.

I ordered the catfish dinner. Sides I chose were hush puppies, Mac & cheese, and cornbread. The sweet tea was authentic, just like my grandmother makes! We also got to sample the lemon cake, which reminded me of key lime pie but with a cake texture. Denverites, go here ASAP.

The hospitality is palpable, the food delectable. I'm going to be a regular for sure!"

6/4/2017 "We've had a lot of BBQ and this is by far the best we've had in Denver! The pulled pork was amazing. The ribs were so good my husband ate them without sauce, and the collards greens are the best I have EVER tasted - and I don't like collard greens. The place is small - mostly food prep with a few chairs and tables for 2 in there. I think it could hold maybe 10-15 people max - in an L shape. So if it's a large group, you should eat outside on the picnic tables or get it to go.

5/29/2017 "Went in again today and it was perfect! We had the Brisket Plate and Rib Plate and all of it was D E L I C I O U S! The counter lady was also totally awesome! EXCELLENT customer service. Thanks for the yummy food and great service! We sat outside and got to smell the smoker and bbq cooking the meat, #heaven ."

5/20/2017 "Lord have mercy, this place is delicious!! Tiny little spot, and there is usually a wait, but everything is prepared to order, and worth every single second. We had brisket, mac and cheese, collards, sweet potatoes and the bread pudding. Everything was amazing. The collard greens are ON POINT! I grew up in the south and hated my Granny's collards so I was reluctant to try these but I'm glad I did- they're delicious! (Sorry, granny) We live fairly close so we will definitely be coming back again and again- great food and a really great story behind their mission. The owner gives back amply to the community. 9news did a story on him and how he helps the homeless as well as to those trying to rebuild their lives after incarceration. So not only do you get ass-smackingly delicious food, you can also feel good about where you are spending your money!"

4/5/2017 "Absolutely amazing. I come from the south east and I know BBQ and Soul. My father owns a smokehouse in South East Ohio and for years now I've been looking for good BBQ here in

Colorado and let me tell you, I'm pretty picky. This place though, it's on point! You're choice of anything on the menu will bring you to a point of down home, mouth -watering goodness."

They bring you traditional fares of collard greens slow cooked with bacon and andouille sausage, mashed potatoes with homemade gravy and slow worked ribs, brisket and pulled pork. Their desserts are out of this world and include sweet potato pie, bread pudding with apples, banana pudding and more.

The chef, lovingly called MO really knows what he's doing and comes to the front to really know you. His kind- hearted nature really shows with the food as he puts his soul into his work, business and over all the cuisine that he puts out.

I'd really suggest stopping in a trying what he has to offer, this will be somewhere I keep going over and over again.

I don't write reviews... Ever really... but this place really got me going. A must have for anyone looking for soul food!

11/13/16 "Mo ended up joining our group and telling us about his journey. His testimony was so inspirational and humbling. Not only is the vibe of this restaurant amazing, the food is also top notch! I ordered the catfish which came with two sides so I got the mac n' cheese and fries. Everything was so satisfying. Best BBQ I've had in Denver!"

2/5/2017
"Daaaaammmmmmmmmmnnnnnnn!!!!! I love me some bbq and soul food. This place is legit. Small place that recently opened in October/ November I think. Only about 5 2 seaters in the restaurant so most people get their food to go. When you first walk into the place, you can smell the delicious aroma of bbq and fried chicken. Owner and the employees are extremely friendly. Service is awesome.

I ordered the brisket dinner plate with mac n cheese and sweet yams. Brisket was soft, tender and delicious. Smokey flavor and decent amount of meat. Loved both the bbq sauce. Mac n cheese was decent..... good flavor but I prefer my mac n cheese to be creamier.

YAMS!!!! Holy!!!! That was my favorite part of the meal.... and I'm usually a meat guy. Sweet, but not overly sweet. Great texture and flavor. Do yourself a favor and order this... you won't regret it. Want to thank the cashier (I think she's the daughter) for recommending it. My gf ordered the fried chicken (dark) with mash potatoes and gravy. I love the fried chicken. Crispy on the outside and tender on the inside. Lots of flavor... I think we got a hint of curry powder. I would come back for the fried chicken. Mash potatoes were just ok.
I think they gave us some hush puppies and those were awesome. Overall, this place is awesome. Wait to get your food is a bit long but it is well worth it. The 2 dinner plates were about $26 and we were both stuffed. I will definitely be back to try everything else. "
Moe ended up joining our group and telling us about his journey. His testimony was so inspirational and humbling. Not only is the vibe of this restaurant amazing, the food is also top notch! I ordered the catfish which came with two sides so I got the mac n' cheese and fries. Everything was so satisfying. Best BBQ I've had in Denver!"

1/6/2017 "Denver's best BBQ! Oh, the meaty goodness! Brisket with beautiful smoke rings, juicy ribs falling off the bone ... I can't wait to try the fried chicken next time, which just might be today or tomorrow. (Writing this is making me salivate, putting my laptop at risk. Not sure if warranty covers drool damage?) I'm thanking the Gods of Gastronomy. I no longer have to go all the way to Castle Rock for fantastic fried chicken. Anointed's fried chicken is going to deliver, I can feel it in my bones. Rib bones ... I'll get some ribs, too, and their current menu, including the Daily Specials. I had one, I but spilled sauce on it, and my DH ate it. For now, here's the one !

6/14/2017 "One of the best eatery experiences I have ever had! The food was PHENOMENAL--best soul food ever! And Mo, the owner, is quite possibly the nicest man on the planet. He truly takes care of you and makes sure you are satisfied. I cant wait to go back!"

News Articles About Anointed BBQ & Soul Food...

9 News Denver Article - May 2017

A New Restaurant owner helping Colorado community

KUSA - A barbecue restaurant near Federal and Hampden is serving up classic soul food dishes and it's drawing big crowds.

Anointed BBQ owner Marriese "Mo" Jones wants his restaurant to do a lot more than just sell food.

Nothing says Sunday afternoon better than friends, barbecue and second helpings.

"You need a little more? " Jones asked one of the customers.

Jones is the man behind Anointed BBQ and Soul Food and he's trying to bring back neighborhood gatherings one roasted pig at a time.

"This is a community restaurant and so we're trying to bring the community together," he said.

One a month the restaurant hosts a gathering where a small donation will get you a plate of food. More than three dozen people showed up to Sunday's event.

"Mo's a saint. I'm telling you. They should sing songs about him," said Gene Ewers.

Ewers is the barbecue joint's newest employee. For him, the restaurant is more than just good food. It's the type of job he's been trying to get for two years.

"When you go to fill out an application and they see 'prison' it's an automatic somethings wrong," he said.

Ewers spent a decade in prison for four DUI's. When he got out, couldn't find employment besides odd jobs.

That is, until he met Jones.

"We don't do handouts, we do hand ups," said Jones.

Jones' goal is to help the homeless and those with criminal records get back on their feet.

"I was a convicted felon. Had a real tough life," he said.

Jones was also homeless for six weeks when he moved to Colorado.

"It was like six years!" he said with a laugh.

He understands just how tough it is to get on the right path when no one will give you the chance.

"I know how it feels to have the door slammed in your face," said Jones.

At his place, a good attitude and wiliness to work will get you a job and maybe even a little more.

"You've got to feed the soul, and you've got to feed the body," he said.

"There are still people out there that will help you, that believes in the good," said Ewers.

It's not just about giving back at the restaurant. Jones and his employees go to homeless shelters once a month and donate a few hours of their time. He says if anyone is looking for a job or just training on how to work in a restaurant, his door is open.

Anointed BBQ and Soul food is located at 2504 West. Hampden Avenue in Denver, Colorado.

Hedges and Highway Outreach Ministries

Hedges and Highway Outreach Ministries (Anointed BBQ's Non-Profit) 501 3 ©

Welcome to H and H, *A MOVEMENT of Great Impact for communities Nationwide.*

Hedges and Highway Outreach Movement is unusual in its outreach!

Actions: Hedges and Highway Outreach Ministries:

- Combats the traditional welfare system. With aims to serve the Denver community since 2006, H and H is a unique outreach ministries helps restore people and rebuild communities utilizing a 50 mile focus and 10 year action plan.

- Provides real solutions for at-risk communities. H & H seeks to *restore historical buildings* (thus beautifying communities) with new vibrant businesses to employ the local people and energize depressed urban areas.

- Mission oriented in our approach, we as the Hedges and Highway Outreach Ministries provide complete community development for people and resources. Each urban area that H & H seeks to restore begins by starting entities that make up what is known as an H & H Life Center. Each "Life Center" is unique to the urban community it serves. **H & H** Life Centers may include entities such as: H & H food and clothing banks, H & H shelters, H & H education centers,

H & H counseling and chaplain services and H & H community businesses (restaurants, delis, bakeries, cafes and coffee shops).

- The goal of H & H Life Centers is to restore peace to urban communities, by giving HOPE for people to have good careers and jobs through education and increased resources.

- Strengthen the local community economic stability EVERY TIME by being strategic and measurable. This will happen by utilizing the "H & H Way" which consists of systems that are proven to achieve results.

- In utilizing these systems, progress is achieved. This includes areas such as job creation, the launch of new community activities, affordable housing options and resources to eliminate homeless in the H & H communities.

Hedges and Highway Outreach Ministries reaches deep into the needs of Sheridan Colorado. Before H & H established a presence at 2504 W. Hamden Avenue, there has not been outreach to Sheridan's over 200 homeless population. Now that Mo and his team have arrived, these residents have a HOPE for their future, which is POWER in their present!!

Our Philosophy; A Hand Up Not a Hand Out

Hedges and Highway Outreach Ministries is a designated 501 (3) (c) and has the vision to serve urban communities through a multitude of transformational services.

Hedges and Highway strengthens other outreaches in our communities creating networks which form our global partnerships of *HOPE*. Committed to empowering people with love, care, spiritual encouragement and education, we feed the natural and spiritual body with well-balanced food.

The H & H design model selects specific ways to approach, systematize and produce results in every urban community that we operate.

Hedges and Highway Outreach Ministries Defenition

- Mission Oriented *in approach (we use the* Centered Set approach to outreach)

- Strategic and Measurable in our systems. (We always utilize the 3 phases of community engagement to address the 3 core values of community development in every area that we operate.)

- Reconciling, redistributing and relocating *people and resources help make the* «H and H Way" consistent as we work with people and communities.

The Vision; Who We Are

Hedges and Highway Outreach Ministries establishes outreach within urban communities at risk. These unique outreaches are multi-faceted and together **create the H and H Life Centers of Reconciliation, Redistribution and Relocation** to make the transformational services tangible.

The H and H Life Centers are collaborations of services and entities with the ultimate goal of **restoring peace to depressed urban areas.**

Our Mission

Hedges and Highway Outreach Ministries is an unusual outreach. Our goal is to serve the nations through our transformational services and a global partnership of HOPE. As we transform the lives of the homeless men, women and youth, H & H Outreach Ministries gives PATHS for people to become productive citizens in their communities. Using a proven results oriented approach, H & H uses the creation of new employment opportunities and increased education to make these changes in people tangible.

As we transform the people, H and H communities of HOPE emerge proving that H & H is UNUSUAL in outreach. H and H has a global focus.

The Values Of H And H

We reconcile people and communities with love, caring and hospitality.

- Intriguing in our multitude of services for everyone that redistribute resources to each community.
- Educational in our programs that redistribute solutions to develop people and local leaders in each community.
- Transforming in our commitment to relocate and live our lives among those we serve.

"The H and H Way"

By Conducting the 3 Phases of engagement EVERYTIME, H and H is consistent & measurable with results. A 2- fold approach is used with 3 Phases of Engagement conducted for every H and H Life Center & urban renewal.

The H and H Life Center concept of creating thriving communities through establishing local restaurant businesses.

We are looking for Volunteers, Missionaries and Outreach Workers.

Outreach workers and Missionaries develop through H and H financial support teams to sustain their living expenses.

Please contact H and H through the contact information at our website for further details!

http://handhcommunityoutreach.weebly.com

About the Author

Marriese Jones, Sr.

"Mo" is the proud owner and founder of ***Anointed BBQ & Soul Food Restaurant*** at 2504 W. Hampden Avenue, Sheridan, Colorado 80110. He owns a non-profit that operates in the Denver Metro area known as **Hedges & Highway: An Unusual Outreach that Serves the Nations through Transformational Services and a Global Partnership of Hope**. Mo is responsible for all operations and management of the company.

Mo brings more than 30 years of expertise in the field of outreach and entrepreneurship. He is educated and experienced in the field of economic community sustainability. Specifically, Mo has worked with the organizations of The Salvation Army, The Denver Rescue Mission and Aurora Mental Health, expanding the PATH homeless initiative for the Aurora Metro area. PATH is Aurora Mental Health's outreach program that was largely non-existent before Mo took hold of birthing the PATH program in Aurora. He has been a business entrepreneur and owner. His past successful ventures include a catering company, a mobile ribs restaurant, seven ice cream trucks and a moo envisions additional restaurants in his future portfolio that will provide avenues for income for the communities which he serves. He has developed a culinary certification program that raises people from poverty to become self-sufficient and successful.

Mo has certificates in outreach that add to his qualifications. He has seen wealth from his organization's revenues and he has experienced homelessness where he worked three jobs to bring his family back to a state of financial wholeness, therefore he can relate to people on every strata of the economic continuum. Now working with business, community and government leaders in the Denver Metro Area for his non-profit Hedges & Highways and has just recently completed a state wide program through Colorado State University. He is part of the seventh graduating class from the Family Leadership Training Institute. Mo leads a viable and successful outreach alongside his flagship restaurant.

Marriese A. Jones Sr. is the 5th child of 6, born and raised in a little town south of Miami called Goulds. If you met "Mo" today, you would most likely comment on his warm smile, his incredible humor and his own "unique way" to draw you in. It is a tendency to think that this guy smiles and laughs too much and just enjoys life! You may wonder if he is ever serious! Marriese A. Jones, Sr. is however, a business man first. Always keeping a watchful eye out to those entrusted to his care, he is never frivolous about the call of God on his life. Serious he is about the ministry and businesses he has birthed and runs, he is a powerful leader of IMPACT and VISION, seeing what is possible for change and then placing strong structures for direct results.

He founded a non-profit called H&H (Hedges and Highway Outreach Ministries) because it conveys the purpose for his life. Marriese saw that everything in my life has led him to this perfect point, where he would lead an organization that reveals a life calling, rather than a mere job. His passion, from the time he was a little boy, has been to care deeply, to the point of action, about the welfare of human beings. As a child, he fought and protected the weaker children. Growing up, he learned to live on his own at the age of only 13. Even then, he can remember cooking for people and inviting them to his apartment to feed and care for them.

Today this is his life. His non-profit has a mission: "Hedges and Highways Outreach Ministries:" An Unusual Outreach that Serves the Nations through Transformational Services and a Global Partnership of Hope."

Marriese is passionate about his progress for those he serves (with H & H) and for his treasured legacies, his many children and grandchildren. His vision is contagious and his leadership solid. Serious is he about these two areas in his life, one will find that in these instances, there is no room for play for Marriese.

Marriese has visions for public policy and to continue his path of being a change agent for the world around him.

Mo has spoken as a guest speaker with Colorado State in October of 2015. He is passionate to share his vision of outreach.

His non-profit, H & H, is based on his call to this ministry as seen in the Scripture of Luke:14:23

"And the Lord said unto the servant, '
'Go out into the highway and hedges
and compel them that my house may be filled.'"

Contact Information

To purchase additional copies of:

40 Years in the Wilderness: the making of a man

and

For Workbook/Group Study: 40 Years in the Wilderness Workbook

Please visit our website:
anointedbbq.com

Marriese A. Jones, Sr. is available
for Speaking Engagements.

Please email us at:
marriesejones40yearsbook@gmail.com
and request a
Speaking Engagement Packet

Made in the USA
Columbia, SC
01 August 2022